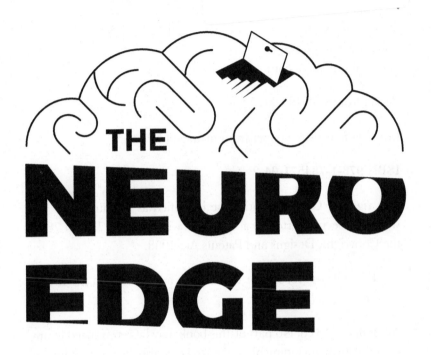

THE NEURO EDGE

People Insights for Leaders and Practitioners

CLIVE HYLAND

The Neuro Edge

First published in 2017 by

Panoma Press Ltd
48 St Vincent Drive, St Albans, Herts, AL1 5SJ, UK
info@panomapress.com
www.panomapress.com

Book layout by Neil Coe.

Printed on acid-free paper from managed forests.

ISBN 978-1-784521-04-2

Printed and bound in Great Britain
by TJ International Ltd, Padstow, Cornwall

DEDICATIONS

To my family, old and new, who continue to inspire me...

Sally

Henry

Chris and Celeste

Suzy and Travis

Tash and Dan

Tara and Kris

Jacob and Louie

Scott, Hannah and Nancy

TESTIMONIALS

"As the leader of a global business I have found huge value in the insights that Clive shares with us in this book. We have worked together for a number of years and I remain impressed by the totality of the material and the way it all seems so relevant to everything we do. It comes together to help me create direction, alignment and a shared cultural language within my organisation. Above all, I value the energetic impact it has on my colleagues: it consistently captivates attention and raises the energy. It opens up important debate by creating a new level of awareness of human nature and behaviour and has enabled me to fully integrate cultural leadership as a cornerstone of the development of my business."

Ronald Spithout, President, Maritime Division, Inmarsat PLC

"Anyone experienced in the challenge of encouraging people to evolve and change will know that an understanding of human dynamics sits at its very core. How we make sense of ourselves and each other is the starting point of any opportunity, enlightenment, enhancement and ultimately alignment of purpose. This book offers us amazing insight into what makes us and defines us. It brings neuroscience into the hands of the layman complete with a tool kit that can add significantly to the ability to influence what goes on around us. Its potential power is truly transformational."

Debbie Jones, Debbie Jones HR

ACKNOWLEDGEMENTS

A huge thank you to my clients, who have shown faith in me and provided the learning experience to help me to put complex concepts into everyday language and context.

Thanks also to my friends and associates who are constantly encouraging me on this exploratory journey.

FOREWORD

Clive and I share a passion for bringing neuroscience into the everyday lives of people and organisations. We believe it can enhance lives if people better understand how they work. Neuroscience is an amazing discipline which is rapidly deepening our understanding.

Being able to integrate the insight from neuroscience with his considerable organisational experience, particularly in the sphere of leadership, is a gift of Clive's. He sees things others do not, and gently opens their eyes.

Brain science can make a major contribution to everyday life and provide a reliable platform for a significantly enhanced understanding of human behaviour.

We get one life and it is precious. Living every day from the perspective that it is a gift, rather than drudgery, is hard for some people. However, good leadership can dramatically improve a person's experience of life. Far too many people are unhappy five out of seven days – and that is crazy. Getting the best out of people involves many things and Clive's insights are a great support to those wanting to excel in this area.

Clive is committed to talking about things at a practical level and equipping people with ideas they can reflect on and utilise. He inspires and challenges. This is a book that can help give people the Neuro Edge.

Amy Brann, Synaptic Potential

Contents

SECTION 1:
THE SCIENCE OF LIFE, THE FUNDAMENTAL PRINCIPLES

SECTION 2:
FURTHER INSIGHTS

SECTION 3:
THE HUMAN ENVIRONMENT

SECTION 4:
PERFORMANCE AND LEADERSHIP

SECTION 5:
REFLECTIONS

CHAPTER 1:

Introduction

All leaders are tasked with the responsibility of getting the most out of their people. Learning and Development and HR professionals share the same goal, albeit more from a supporting perspective. It is my total conviction that neuroscience offers incredibly powerful insights as to how our understanding of this challenge can be taken to another level.

Ultimately this book, for me, is optimistic; not some groundless optimism based purely on wishful thinking, but one centred on the new levels of human understanding emerging through the development of neuroscience. It is not a science book as such, although scientific principles will be explored throughout. More importantly, it is an attempt to bring the power and relevance of this subject area into everyday life and business practice.

Summarising a subject as deep and wide as neuroscience is like flying over an ocean. You can get some sense of its vast power and expanse but there are always questions about what is going on below the surface. This book starts the journey of exploring some of these depths. Writing the book has been an important experience for me. For some time I have *felt* the power and importance of the subject and, indeed, when I do public or organisational presentations I get consistently positive feedback about the passion I display. Yet assembling this next stage of the jigsaw puzzle has taken me to a significantly deeper level of understanding and belief. The process of laying out the pieces of my knowledge before me and assembling them into something approaching a coherent whole, combined with finding the required discipline and focus to ensure the work is ready for public scrutiny, has been cathartic and satisfying in its own right. Yet the journey continues.

After studying sociology and psychology in my early career, I have invested considerable time examining neuroscientific literature and research material and networking with highly competent specialists to build my knowledge. I have been using its underlying principles for over 10 years as a leadership coach. This has taken me into business and organisational practice, personal coaching, sporting performance, faith, families and prisons. Now it feels like everything I do is underpinned by the insights I will share with you across these pages. I see its relevance every day and everywhere.

We all see and experience other people's behaviour but analysis at the behavioural level alone is superficial. This book will explore what drives our behaviour, what is the source rather than just the outcome.

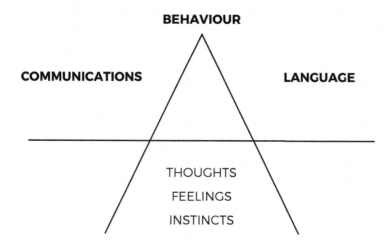

Many of us are familiar with the iceberg model which shows behaviour as something visible above the surface of the water, but most of us would accept that behaviour itself is a product of the human dynamics that are going on below the surface, including thoughts, feelings and instincts. Somebody labelled an introvert may behave in such a way because they feel only minimal need for the company of others or because they are afraid of others and do not know how to express themselves. The former may be entirely happy with their style; the latter may feel lonely and isolated. So, if we are interested in supporting behavioural change or advancement, we need to go below the surface to understand what triggers human behaviour, what makes us behave the way we do.

For me, psychology has offered amazing insights on this, but ultimately it remains vulnerable to the limitations of an observational model, that is it relies on theoretical models built through establishing correlations between observed human behaviour and possible 'mind-based' triggers and responses. There was really no alternative for a discipline which flourished in the 20th century and which did not have the advantages of modern technologies to expand its learning further. Meanwhile, neuroscience has undergone a fundamental transition. Much of the research in the 20th century centred on the study of mammals, such as rats and monkeys. The extent to which this was immediately relevant to human behaviour was always to some degree an unknown. This has fundamentally changed in the 21st century, especially through the development of advanced imaging technology, such as functional MRI scanning. Now, neuroscientists are able to watch live human brains in action. We have moved from building 'theories of mind' from outside the brain to building knowledge of the brain itself from the inside.

The journey of understanding exactly how our brains work has well and truly begun and, in my opinion, will become an irresistible force in the decades ahead. Meanwhile, whilst the neuroscience profession itself continues to apply its vast talent and growing resources to further this field of highly specialised and rigorous study, we as lay people can afford ourselves the opportunity to start integrating the emerging knowledge with our own experience of life and begin to reap its benefits immediately. Much of the fruit is already ripe for consumption and it's too good to waste.

I am deeply indebted to all whose research I have studied and to immense books written by people such as Joseph LeDoux, Matt Lieberman, Dan Siegel, Tim Gallwey, Daniel Goldman and Paul Ekman.

The first section will lay down the key scientific principles that I believe everyone should be aware of and will therefore form the basis for the rest of the book. In the second section I will examine these principles in more depth. In Section 3 I will examine how these principles play out in our everyday lives within the human environment we have created. Section 4 will focus more specifically on human performance and leadership. Section 5 is a shorter reflective commentary and will include some 'bigger picture' observations.

Occasionally I will be embedding some of the insights I share in my own personal experiences. This is, after all, an attempted explanation of what may be going on inside our heads and our hearts. In this sense, at least, some of it is an explanation from the inside out. Whilst each of our personal stories are different, I hope that sharing some aspects of mine will resonate with you and help you to further understand the lessons of your own life so far. I hope it offers you understanding, enlightenment and a rich platform for the personal choices you will be making in the future.

SECTION 1:
THE SCIENCE OF LIFE, THE FUNDAMENTAL PRINCIPLES

CHAPTER 1.1:

Key Insights

I would ask you at the outset to consider the fundamental insights highlighted below. They are potentially life-changing. The enormity of their impact might strike you instantly or it may take time. If you connect immediately with their message, this is a great starting place and I hope the rest of the book will give you the opportunity to add depth and clarity to your initial intuitive response. If you read these opening statements with curiosity but still remain 'on the fence' I urge you to continue with the remainder of the text as I set out to bring the insights alive through the tapestry of our everyday lives. These are the headlines, the content will follow.

Why is this important? This is because so much of the human brain remains an untapped resource. By exploring the true wonder of the brain we can open our eyes to the fantastic opportunities it offers us both now and in the future to enrich our own lives and the lives of others.

1: THE CONNECTIVITY OF THE HUMAN BRAIN

What an amazing 'machine' the human brain is: a wonderful bundle of intense electrical circuitry and biochemical activity, weighing approximately three pounds and needing 60 watts of energy to function. It consists of approximately 90 billion neurons (brain cells), each having a capacity to connect with other neurons

10,000 times. Each of these connections will play a role in the vast array of thoughts, feelings and instincts we will experience throughout our lives.

It is quite something to imagine electrical circuitry of this size compressed into such a small space. Yet it is the multiplicity of connection that is key: this is the synaptic potential of the brain. The synapses are the points of electrical connectivity across the neural pathways of the brain enabled by chemical activity. This connection is created by neurotransmitters – the brain's hormones and chemical messengers facilitating the flow of electrical currents. There are approximately one billion synapses for every cubic centimetre of the brain.

Imagine having built a machine that could turn on and off every one of its 90 billion connections according to need and immediately reconnect to any one of 10,000 other circuits! And all 'wrapped' in the most amazing intelligent software which allows it to self-learn, self-direct and self-heal. Each of us carries our own unique brain with us wherever we go, yet we understand so little about how it operates. It's time to change this.

2: THE TRIUNE BRAIN

Most of us are broadly familiar with the distinctions of the left and right-sided brain. There is a more powerful insight: that of the 'triune brain'. This refers to the three layers of the brain, each of which evolved for distinctly different purposes. These are:

-    The basal region: the oldest part of the brain, sitting just above the brain stem and often referred to as the reptilian brain.

-    The limbic system: the middle region of the brain, also known as the mammalian brain.

- The cortex: the top layer and the youngest in evolutionary terms. We can loosely call this the human region of the brain.

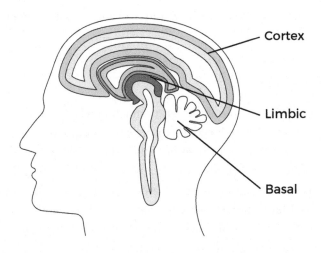

By understanding the evolutionary purpose of each of these regions we have an opportunity to look again at who we really are, how we function and how we are currently using, or not using, the vast expanse of brain talent that is available to us.

3: THE ROLE OF THE CORTEX

We can broadly think of the human cortex (the top layer of the brain) as the thinking brain. It is the region of the brain which we associate with logical rules and rational data processing and is the basis of our conscious reasoning. Yet it accounts for only about 20% of the total connectivity of the brain. In effect this is 20% of the brain's intelligence.

So what about the remaining 80%? If it is not conscious and it's not logical, what is it? This is the largely unconscious world of the limbic and basal regions. Any attempt to restrict our understanding of human nature to approaches which assume conscious logical processing as the primary feature of the operation of the brain will miss significant insights. We need to tap into the deeper worlds of the limbic and basal layers of the brain to reconnect with an inner intelligence that seems to have often evaded acknowledgement over recent centuries.

4: EMOTIONS

Emotions are registered in the brain much quicker than thoughts. It takes around 80 milliseconds to register an emotion compared with 250 milliseconds to register a thought. In the world of the amazing processing speeds of the brain this difference is significant. It means that our thoughts are always trying to catch up with our emotions. Our instantaneous experience of life is emotional. Our thoughts then help us to understand what has just happened and aid us to build thought structures and patterns so that we can make ongoing sense of our lives.

The implications of this are enormous. So much traditional science has assumed that our thoughts are the driving force of our behaviour. Emotions were too difficult to explain and were left beneath the radar of scientific enquiry. Now the paradigm is being reversed. Emotions are both the source of our life's experience and the primary drivers in much of our behaviour. Emotions need to be understood at source.

5: ENERGY

We experience emotions as an energetic sensation in the body. Within this context, it therefore follows that we need to understand energy and how it impacts us. More precisely it means delving into the world of universal energy and bringing it to the theatre of human understanding with the same degree of reverence as any social science or psychology based discipline. Every living organism, including human beings, is an energy system in its own right and forms part of the vast tapestry of energy we call the universe.

We are all energetic creations which have become manifest at a level of vibration where mass is formed. Equally, the space between us is in fact not space at all (in the sense of implying 'nothingness'); it is a dynamic universe of constant energetic transactions. We are not individually sealed away from the universe. It is not external to us, it is a central part of our being; each of us was created by a combination of the elements formed by the stars themselves. To fail to understand how energy impacts our life experience is like hiding our heads in the sand.

6: INSTINCTS

The deepest and oldest part of the brain is the basal region. It served our evolutionary ancestors long before we developed human or even mammalian form, yet today it is still in many ways the powerhouse of the brain. This is the domain of human instincts. When our instincts are engaged the rest of the brain follows – no fuss, no negotiation. It is a world of speed of response and decisive action and sits at the heart of the survival of our species. Yet it is deep, dark and often inaccessible. It is impressionist rather than precise and big picture rather than detail. It is the boss. If there are perceived issues of survival at stake or, indeed, a fundamental opportunity to thrive, our instincts will take the wheel and guide us in the moment. Any attempt to understand human behaviour without grasping every opportunity to learn about this deeper world of brain activity is inevitably built on dangerously shaky foundations.

7: NATURE V NURTURE

Connectivity is the essence of our brain's intelligence. We have around 90 billion neurons, each capable of connecting 10,000 times. When we are born we have all the connective capacity we will ever need. Our new brains are like a universe of potential. They have the capability to take us well beyond the limitations of our current thinking. Yet the newly born brain is not connected up. It is our experience of life that will determine this connectivity.

From the outset, our brains will react to life experience by creating the neurological connections deemed necessary to survive and thrive. A fixed brain template would be too inflexible and incapable of optimising human response to the huge variation of circumstances that life can present us. So our brains arrive with massive potential; our early life experiences will then lay down the foundation 'blueprints' to help us cope with the world we are experiencing. In turn, these highly personalised blueprints will hold strong sway over how we will react throughout life.

Understanding the dynamics of 'nature versus nurture' is fundamental to the subject matter of this book.

8: THE WIDER HUMAN INTELLIGENCE SYSTEM

The brain does not control the heart. It is not a master-slave relationship; rather, they act as partners swapping intelligence to optimise the response and development of the total organism. In many circumstances, the heart sends more instructions to the brain than vice-versa. The heart plays a vital role in the overall human intelligence system and its role is particularly significant in understanding areas such as mindfulness, meaningful human connection and confidence. It is a fundamental player in bringing meaning to our lives.

Similarly, the intelligence system which sits within the gut (our enteric system) plays a key role in our instinctive responses.

Human intelligence needs to be understood well beyond the dynamics of the cranial brain. It is a total brain and body system.

9: EMOTIONS AND CONSCIOUSNESS

Here we discover a fundamental contradiction. Our emotional experiences and the memories attached to them are fundamental drivers in our experience of life and our behaviour. Yet, important aspects of our emotional history are not accessible by conscious analysis and reflection. This means that to some degree each person's life is a constant roller coaster between conscious thoughts and unconscious feelings, the only certainty being that they are never entirely reconcilable.

Where does this leave us? Does this mean we are all resigned largely to being victims of our unconscious emotions? And how can we address this moving forward?

CHAPTER 1.2:

The Evolution Of The Triune Brain

Having introduced the concept of the triune brain in the last chapter, we need now to look at this in more depth and especially from an evolutionary perspective. Here we are primarily concerned with insights which help us to understand how the brain directs our behaviour. Of course, it does more than this, from the fundamental operating of our body, such as breathing and heart rate, to the functioning of all five senses, the processing of sight, sound, smell, touch and taste. However, for the main focus of this book we will confine our interest largely to understanding what it is that causes us to think, feel and behave the way we do.

PHASE 1: THE BASAL REGION (THE REPTILIAN BRAIN)

Biologically, this is the autopilot of the brain responsible for many of the body's internal processes, which operate well away from our conscious awareness, such as breathing, blood circulation, digestion and balance.

To understand the essential purpose and role of this region of the brain from a behavioural perspective it is useful to reflect on the basic functioning of reptiles themselves. The basal region is referred to as the reptilian brain for very good reasons. Reptiles represent the first evolutionary phase when mobile life forms roamed the lands of the earth millions of years ago, including the great prehistoric creatures that often take star billing in so many movies. But it is probably more helpful to use a modern example of a reptile to illustrate the relevant points here.

Consider the crocodile, the proven survivor of many millennia that still flourishes in the modern world. The one thing the crocodile understands above all else is how to survive. Its response to environmental triggers is essentially instinctive. It responds with speed and decisiveness – no fuss, no meandering. If its survival is at stake it will act with impressive speed and power. If it senses an opportunity to kill it will focus on nothing else until the deed is done.

Crocodiles don't 'do' relationships. The only time they collaborate with other crocodiles is to tear flesh or execute a collective kill. You cannot train them. If there is no survive or thrive stimulus, they are not engaged and cannot be enticed to do so. Crocodiles spend their lives primarily executing the kills they need to survive or absorbing the sun's energy to prepare for the next kill.

Their parenting instincts are negligible. Soft eggs are laid on land and their offspring are allowed to stick around for a very short period of about three months. If the young outlive their welcome they become just another food target and will be eaten by the parents that created them. It is a story of the survival of the species in its rawest form: no frills or distractions, just a focus on doing only what is needed to be done to survive.

And so it is with the basal region of the human brain today. Whilst no layer of the brain operates in isolation from the whole, the essential purpose of this part of the brain in a behavioural sense is to secure the survival of the organism. It responds quickly and decisively to matters that threaten its very existence or to fundamental opportunities to thrive. When the basal region of the brain decides to engage, the rest of the brain follows. It makes decisions without hesitation and does so in the belief that it is doing what is right to secure its own future.

Yet it is also quite lazy. If it senses no survival relevance it will not want to engage and will happily 'delegate' serious processing work to the other brain regions. It does not concern itself with detail or emotional nicety as these are not seen as fundamental matters of survival. It is territorial and highly protective of what it perceives to be its own sphere of operation.

As its existence has pre-dated more recent evolutionary phases, it works with primal sensory data, with that of sight, smell, sound, touch and taste. As seeing is the primary sense in humans with the power to override all the others, it is highly dependent on visual data, whether external images gathered from the outside world or indeed subjective images constructed through internal visualisation.

'Seeing is believing' is indeed a valid statement, a requirement for human engagement at a meaningful level. You may not engage the instinctive brain with spoken or written word alone, a subject we will return to in more depth later in the book.

PHASE 2: THE LIMBIC SYSTEM (THE MAMMALIAN BRAIN)

As evolution progressed, particularly through the cataclysmic events that saw the end of the dinosaurs, it took on a significant new phase in the development of the brain. This was the evolution of the brain's limbic system, especially in mammals. Evolution had 'worked out' that survival in the harsh climatic conditions of land called for another type of capability that was not significantly evident in reptiles. This was the ability to cooperate.

The limbic system of the brain was evolved specifically to enable mammals to cooperate in numbers and to build social groupings for the first time. Hence, the emergence of families and parenting instincts built on the understanding that the species had a better chance of survival by operating in groups. As we have seen, reptiles do not operate this way. Now, evolution was building a limbic system that would enable a far more sophisticated level of connection between mammals, thereby creating the capability for a collective response to the challenges of the environment.

Most obviously this occurred in the development of observable communication techniques. Mammals took the sophistication of social interaction to another level. Reptiles demonstrate an acute sensitivity to the movement of other creatures and to the most basic sensations, such as fear, but mammals developed more complex social interactions and structures with hierarchies of privilege and importance. Think of monkeys and the functioning of their communities as clear examples of social cooperation. This is evidenced openly at the behavioural level. Monkeys, like other mammals, have developed clear patterns of behaviour for demonstrating assertion or submission, courage or fear, and authority and allegiance – all vital elements to a functioning community. These will range from grunts and noises, to exhibitions of aggression or beauty, to varieties of body posture and positioning.

Yet, there was something less observable going on. To fully understand this we have to remind ourselves that evolving mammals had no spoken language to share and whilst some of the observable behaviour described above was useful, there was so much more that could be done to intensify the process of social bonding. If spoken language was not available to build communication then they needed another means of communication. The natural communication medium available to them was energy.

The limbic region of the brain is designed to be highly tuned energetically to other mammals to the extent that it can directly sense and, to some degree, experience their mood and energy. Energy plays a key role in any emotional connection we feel with others, whether positive or negative. It is contagious, a transaction we can share on an energetic level. Indeed, whilst we will return to this subject in greater depth later in the book, for now we can think of emotions as being essentially energetic reactions experienced in our bodies. So, from an evolutionary perspective, to become more aware of the emotional sensations of others of our species opened up a whole new opportunity for bonding and interaction. The limbic region of the brain has evolved highly complex machinery for enabling this connection.

Mammals cannot only see the response of other mammals, they have the capability to *feel* it. The so-called 'resonance circuitry', which sits in this part of the brain, gives mammals the capability to 'read' not only the behaviour of other mammals but also to sense their mood. This is done by recreating in their own brain what it perceives is happening in the brain of others. This 'reading' is translated into our own internal experience so we not only recognise the signals but also feel the sensation. Communication was now not just instinctive but was also emotional.

We will further discuss this area of resonance circuitry in humans later. For now it is important to understand that mammals had evolved beyond the purely instinctive interaction of reptiles to that of a more sophisticated emotional connection. This meant that more complex and effective interaction was possible, thus paving the way for more sophisticated social structures where the survival of the species was directly entwined with its ability to act in groups.

Furthermore, the evolutionary legacy of this emotional evolution was just as significant for the human species. This depth of human connection was to become a fundamental feature in our experience of life itself. When we look more closely later at the necessity for human bonding we will see just how fundamentally important this is to our lives.

The limbic system is therefore the centre of our emotional world and the source of our relationships. We have seen here that energetic connection gave mammals the means to communicate, but what about the motivation to do so? For mammals, this desire was no longer built just on a raw need for individual survival. They developed a fundamental need for relationships, to be part of an interactive dynamic whereby one's whole life experience is enriched by social and emotional connection with others. For mammals there is no choice: they need each other. Evolution has demanded it.

PHASE 3: THE CORTEX (THE "HUMAN" BRAIN)

In loosely calling the cortex, the top layer of the brain, the 'human' brain it does not imply that we are the only species that has one, but, by comparison, there is no other species that has a brain cortex that can go anywhere near the human cortex for sophistication and functionality. We are in a league all of our own. There is nothing different about human brains in terms of design principles which set us apart from our evolutionary path; it is more that our brains are examples of larger primate brains where brain capacity to body mass far outweighs that of other species. Evolution worked out that accelerated development of this part of the brain would deliver far more significant dividends than other parts of our anatomy. And, above all, it is the neo-cortex (the 'modern cortex') which sets us apart from all other life forms and enabled us to dominate the planet. So what is so special about it?

The cortex, amongst other vital functions, is the centre of our thinking ability and its evolutionary development has given humans the ability to consider the impact of their emotions and instincts and to stand back from simply being driven by them. Beware, ultimately our instincts and emotions are still more powerful than our thoughts and will dictate our responses in many circumstances. Yet, as humans, through the development of thought we have given ourselves a much wider set of choices. We are no longer simply slaves to emotional and instinctive stimuli and response. Now we have developed the capability of conscious awareness and choice.

As stated earlier, thoughts are triggered more slowly in the brain than emotions. Our thoughts are there to help us understand what has happened when we experience emotional and instinctive reactions. Without this, we would simply carry on responding in the same manner with only the most basic level of learning. Yet humans have learnt to think about their actions and gradually to consider wider optional responses the next time they are presented with the same stimuli. In this sense we developed the ability to pause momentarily and make choices before we react to all but the more powerful emotional triggers.

You will have experienced this for yourself in your daily life. You will have felt an emotional reaction within your body, such as feeling threatened or hurt, and you will typically try to give yourself a little reflective time to work out what has just happened before you express your response. We are doing this all the time but mostly we are not very aware of it, but when the emotional stakes are raised the reactive process becomes a lot clearer. How many times have we reacted immediately through anger only to start realising almost as quickly that our response was not the wisest choice in the given circumstances? Indeed, much of human life itself is a journey of reflective navigation through the emotional roller coasters that we encounter along the way.

So, as our data bank of reflective learning increased, the evolving neo-cortex became the region of the brain where we developed the conscious rules for our existence. It is where we lay down the neural pathways that are triggered as conscious activity in the brain. It therefore became the regional neuro centre for non-emotional activity such as logic, structure, method, facts, details and process. Whereas the limbic brain is the source of our personal subjective experience, the cortex seeks to become the domain of objective analysis and external fact.

This continued evolution of the cortex in time resulted in a particularly significant capability which has set us apart so clearly from all other species: this is the concept of *future*. All reptiles and mammals have a concept of the past built into memory and simple observation will demonstrate clearly that they live their lives in the present. They do not, however, think about the future. They do not plan other than at a very basic instinctive level. On the other hand, humans are preoccupied with the future, whether it is a simple mental rehearsal in our heads of the words we intend to express before we share them, or, at the other extreme, being concerned with the livelihoods of our loved ones after our deaths. We are constantly creating a view of the future in our minds so that we can navigate our choices at a conscious level. As a species we stand alone in our ability to do this.

So, why did we develop this capability? Because it worked! It was an essential step in taking control of our environment. Compare the learning styles of the mammal and human. Learning for the mammal is very basic and based on observation and repetition. A monkey will watch another perform tasks and will then copy those actions if it sees a potential reward. If it succeeds it will do the same thing again; if it fails it won't bother. The human brain took this technique to a whole new level. Now the thinking is more like: if I do this, this, this and this then I get this result. Now it can project a sequence of actions and a likely consequence. The human has uniquely introduced the ability to plan and with this comes the acknowledgement of future and our ability to influence it.

Combining the thinking ability of the cortex and the cooperative dynamics of the limbic system placed humans in a very powerful position to take control of their territories. Initially this would be the human tribe outmanoeuvring the animals in their locality; now we see this dominance expressed on a global scale.

So far, so good for the human species. But of course this is not the whole story. Whilst this ability to plan for the future massively served the human ability to survive, it brought with it a much less obvious challenge. The acknowledgement of future meant that we were seeing life as a journey with a beginning and an end and this increasingly posed huge existential questions for us. If life was a journey, then what was its purpose? What was the meaning of life itself?

Our ability to stand back and look in on ourselves, combined with our increasing capacity for considering the bigger picture, meant that we would remain entranced by the wonders of our environment. Evolution has guided us to understand how we fit into the world in which we live. The purpose of this was to work out how we pursued our best chance of survival. In earlier times our awareness extended only to what we immediately saw before us. Yet, even Stone Age man appears to have been intrigued by the existence of the stars in his sky. In the modern era, our awareness of our environment has extended well beyond our planetary boundaries out into the outer reaches of the universe. Yet, we are still asking the question 'what lies beyond?' Herein lies our fundamental need to understand our role in our environment. We cannot ignore uncertainty in our environment and are always drawn to bringing it under our sphere of control.

So, as humans we will always seek out the purpose for any action that we consider. As reptiles there was very little conscious choice, it was more a matter of instinctive reaction. But now our sophisticated brain maintains the search for purpose not only at the pragmatic level but also in terms of the search for life meaning. An animal with no significant sense of self would not be drawn to answering questions about the meaning of its existence. But as humans we have no choice; we have self-awareness and are very conscious of our own boundaries and those of our world. Our own personal life meaning depends substantially on how we experience and make sense of the interaction across these boundaries.

For the increasingly complex human brain this search for purpose has translated into asking the fundamental question 'why?' What is the purpose of anything we do and how does it help me to survive? From the most basic reasons for carrying out tasks to the big life-purpose questions, searching out an answer to the question 'why?' sits at the heart of human meaning and motivation.

This is a subject that will feature strongly in later chapters in this book as we especially consider subjects like belief and spirituality, but for now we can at least recognise the evolutionary context in which the search for meaning and purpose has become such a pronounced feature of the human journey.

CHAPTER 1.3:

Brain Development and Life's Journey

"We are all faced with a series of great opportunities brilliantly disguised as impossible situations."

– Charles R Swindoll

This chapter will look at how our brains develop throughout our lives, from initial conception to eventual decline. It will include the discussion about 'nature v nurture'.

CREATION AND INSTINCTS

From the point of conception, our brains start to develop in our mother's womb, beginning with the brain stem. The unborn baby will soon sense its immediate environment and its initial brain development will already be influenced by the demeanour and activity of its mother. If the mother is relaxed, calm and generally enjoying the pregnancy, this will facilitate the baby's healthy development. In effect, the baby is being primed to get ready for a supportive and nurturing world. Consequently, those parts of the brain concerned with such nurturing and support will accelerate their development.

On the other hand, if the mother is stressed, volatile and generally finding the pregnancy distressing, the baby will begin preparing for a hostile world and those parts of the brain concerned with survival and defence will accelerate their development.

Then comes the birth. At the time of birth the human brain has all the potential it will need to take on life's journey. All the fundamental neural 'wiring' is in place but much of it is not yet connected up. Consider that each of the brain's 90 billion neurons is capable of connecting around 10,000 times and it is this amazing connectivity that will enable the brain to develop and adapt to the environment it is born into. In this sense, the newly born brain is like a newly purchased software program. It has potential but it cannot function in the intended way without data, like a spreadsheet with no figures. It is life's experience which provides the data. As the baby accumulates experience it will connect up the neural circuitry of the brain to respond to its experiences and its environment.

The parents themselves will undergo hormonal changes to reinforce the bond with the baby. For Mum this has been going on throughout the pregnancy and will intensify at the point of birth. This bonding is not just hormonal (biochemical), it is also reinforced by the baby's proximity to the mother's heart in the womb. The heart itself creates electromagnetic waves which will act to sooth the developing baby (assuming Mum is in a reasonable emotional state) as it directly resonates with its newly formed heart. This applies throughout the pregnancy and will continue to act as a source of comfort beyond birth. It is this 'magical' electromagnetic connection which is a vital element of the post-natal bonding process as the baby seeks the familiarity of the heartbeat that has been its ever-present source of comfort throughout its life in the womb. No surprise then that being cuddled close to the heart is such a pacifying process for the newly born and infant alike.

Likewise, Dad himself will undergo hormonal changes at the point of birth. It may be less obvious than Mum but there is growing evidence that the more Dad is exposed to the pre-birth and actual birth experience, the more his own hormonal make-up will change to reinforce the nurturing connection with the baby. Additionally, direct tactile exchange between baby and Dad, such as direct skin to skin contact, will further increase the sensory alignment between the two and further reinforce their connection. Let's face it, is there anything more emotionally powerful than cuddling the baby you have created? Winners all round – Mum, Dad and baby! Yet this is not just an emotional desire, it is a function of genetic design which ensures the maximum chances of the baby's survival in its new world.

Here we are uncovering the nature v nurture debate. For nature we can think of the circuitry of the newly created brain as the genetic template that we have inherited from our parents through their DNA. They will have passed on specific genetic formulas which will not only determine such things as the way we look but also give us an inbuilt predisposition to the way we will react to the world. For instance, if we have been born to tough, industrious parents it is more than likely that we will have a level of inbuilt resilience to support us through life.

Yet this is only the start of the story. Our genes continue to express themselves throughout our lives so that the brain is never static in its development. This is where the nurture side comes into play. Our life experiences will directly nurture and guide the developing connectivity of the brain. The brain works broadly on the principle of 'use it or lose it', so the more we are exposed to a world of empathy and constructive relationships, the more we will connect up the pathways concerned with advancing these capabilities. The more we are exposed to threat and violence, the more the brain will reinforce the connectivity needed for defence and survival.

The same applies to execution skills. The brain of a concert pianist will have developed to master the dexterity and rhythm of his profession. This will be very different from the brain development of an individual who has had no opportunity or encouragement to learn skills of artistic expression. If all the individual has experienced is threat and neglect, his brain cannot understand anything different. This is another core theme I will return to later in the book.

There is a heuristic (rule of thumb) we can use here: the earlier the influence on the developing brain, the more powerful and long-lasting the impact. Let's examine this further.

The early brain is like a blank piece of paper. Everything is to be learnt, nothing needs to be unlearnt. The newly born baby will already have certain instinctive instructions activated on arrival, such as the need to cry. This is less about being upset and is more a mechanism for attracting attention. The baby knows it cannot survive on its own; it needs others to react and so the cry is pitched at the perfect level to ensure it is not ignored. It is a survival imperative. For the first three months after birth, a baby's behaviour is almost entirely driven by its genetic instincts. The basal (instinctive) region of the brain has been in place from the earliest development in the womb.

The emotional brain, however, is very much in catch-up. New connectivity is created in the brain at a rate of around half a million connections per second in these early months as it soaks up the environmental data needed to thrive. This includes sensing intelligence about its relationship with its parents or primary care givers. It is vital that the baby works out very early on how to master these critical relationships and this is where the emotional brain (the limbic region) really comes into its own.

AGE 3 MONTHS TO 3 YEARS: THE DEVELOPMENT OF THE EMOTIONAL BRAIN

The development of the limbic region of the brain really starts to demonstrably kick in at about three months and will be the primary source of visible behavioural development until about three years of age.

This is where the baby really starts to create the emotional connections with its parents at a deeper level and where it will learn to exhibit behaviours which will strengthen the emotional bond. Whilst the instinctive stage has done everything it can to ensure the baby's survival, it is time now to enrich the experience of life itself and to create the relationships that matter most.

Of course, parents (or primary care givers) will continue to be vital to the baby's ongoing survival, but their role is much more significant than just this. For all of us, our primary experience of life is through our emotions, the immediate and accumulated sensations of life that we experience throughout our bodies. And it is our parents that are the providers of the greatest emotional experiences that will influence the development of our brains at this critical formative time. A baby can only learn at this stage by seeing or experiencing.

Parents have the opportunity to help their baby to create the emotional capability to love, to trust and to experience joy and happiness, to directly feel the bond of caring relationships and the connection with those who love us. Equally, the 'wrong' parenting, or even the absence of good parenting, can create an emotional template within the baby that is more tuned to fear, threat, rejection and isolation. A baby does not yet have the capacity to analyse these experiences but will feel them all the same. In fact, the experience is probably deeper since it doesn't have the rationalisation capability to make sense of what is going on.

This stage of brain development largely pre-dates cognitive memory, so significant emotional experiences here, whilst fundamental in shaping the baby's view of life, will frequently not be accessible to conscious recall in the future. Likewise, emotional difficulties created here will not be easily accessible to cognitive therapeutic influence if they need to be revisited in later life. The cognitive neural pathways which facilitate conscious memory and recall will not yet have been sufficiently laid, so whilst our emotional memories are always with us they can remain deep below the layer of conscious awareness.

A baby's learning ability at this stage is very much based on watching and copying. Both mirroring and resonance circuitry (which we will look at further later) is developing in the brain at an amazing speed and the baby will become more and more proficient at replaying the postures and gestures that attract the desired attention. These are no longer just instinctive gestures delivered robotically in compliance with genetic programming; now they are becoming real feelings exposing both brain and body to the sensations of meaningful human connection.

For the first two years of its development the brain has been ramping up its connectivity, almost without discretion or choice. It is hungry for data and, as yet, does not have the mechanisms for selection that will start to appear shortly. The toddler's brain will extend its connective capacity to as much as 15,000 connections per neuron by the age of two. Then, it will begin to exercise discretion as the brain strengthens the connections which experience has taught it to value, while at the same time allowing less important connections to lapse and fade. This natural process of neural pruning will be essential to the optimisation of its neural activity throughout life.

And so this process of deepening connection with its parents will continue and the baby will become increasingly adept at both recognising and communicating the social cues and signals which will help the family unit to support one another at the behavioural level. Young babies are constantly searching out who they can and cannot trust; their instincts tell them that their life depends on it. Yet they have to do so without the explicit help of rational processes. Instead it is the integrated work of the instinctive and emotional systems which combine to sense safety or threat.

As we are likely to have experienced, babies are very sensitive to body language and movement. They will pick up very quickly on our mood and energy and respond accordingly. Similarly, this is also the time when babies are in effect learning the skills of 'mind-reading', largely via the medium of the facial expressions of their parents. They will increasingly share a subconscious understanding of each other without needing recourse to rational thought processes. The connection is just there and works without conscious manipulation.

I recognise that there is a danger here that I appear to be presenting the early parenting experience through rosy spectacles as a period of faultless alignment and mutual understanding. Far from it! As any parent knows, it is not at all easy and would be readily described by most as a very challenging and emotional time. Of course it is. Both baby and parents are going through fundamental changes to their biochemistry and their experience base. This period is indeed characterised by raw emotions. What I have done above is simply explain how that bonding and understanding process has to evolve to allow these formative relationship years to be navigated with as much success as possible. It is, at the same time, a wonderful, loving, scary and anxious period and its purpose is to create a suitable emotional capacity in a baby's brain to be ready for the first lap of life's journey.

AGE 3+: THE DEVELOPMENT OF THE COGNITIVE BRAIN

Whilst these timescales should not be regarded as rigid, they are a useful general indicator of when the maturing cortex will come to the fore in the child's development. Having navigated the instinctive and emotional phases of development, it is now time to accelerate our thinking capability.

As we have indicated earlier, the human neo-cortex stands alone from other species in terms of its degree of sophistication. It is the region of the brain which thrives on logic and structure and on method and process. Essentially it is the area of the brain where we learn and capture the conscious rules for living our lives, ranging from task execution to those of social engagement. Whilst we feel social interaction through the limbic system, the experience is raised to our level of conscious awareness through the thinking cortex.

The neural circuitry of the cortex works on digital principles. The synaptic connections which create the connectivity of the thinking brain can be considered as decision gateways which will determine where electrical impulses will be directed step by step along their journey. The circuits which are fired up by each and every impulse are in fact the neural source of our conscious reactions.

So it is entirely fitting that the child increasingly uses this newly emerging cognitive capacity to try to build its own conscious understanding of what life is about. A key element of this is language. Whilst the child will have already picked up simple language before the age of three, it is now destined to become a vital medium for making sense of the world.

Language itself is a structure, a set of rules encapsulating the verbal and written expressions which enable a more precise level of everyday personal and collective meaning to be shared throughout our lives. Not only is it a pragmatic interpersonal communication mechanism but it will increasingly influence the shaping of our thoughts. Imagine the difficulty of trying to reflect on an experience without the aid of language. Whilst there is undoubtedly a level of instinctive and emotional processing underpinning our experiences, it is the functionality of the cortex which lifts this to a conscious level. It is then at this conscious level that advanced learning can take place. And so it is appropriate that our growing child is now rapidly approaching mandatory schooling age. Its brain is ready for formalised education.

AGE 5 to 12 AND THE EDUCATION SYSTEM

In most modernised education systems, teaching focuses mainly on intellectual development. The pupil's brain will gradually be taught how to follow the rules of learning and to capture this in written and verbal form. There will be significant exposure to methods and techniques, to numbers, to processing and to the external validation of learning.

The examination process is, of course, the classic representation of this. Simplistically, pupils are told what to learn and they have to prove that they have indeed learnt it, typically by the written evidence of a structured examination. The scrutiny of external assessment then stays with them for the rest of their educational careers, ideally culminating in formal qualifications which can be used to support occupational careers.

Of course, this is not the full story of school-based learning. There will also be art subjects encouraging varying levels of subjective expression but even these will be measured not by the nature of the student's experience but by the evidence of examination success. And then there is the significant parallel path of social learning also being followed over the same period: the behavioural rules of how to engage with others, whether that means teacher, officials, playground friends or, indeed, playground enemies. This is the informal or pastoral learning experience that will probably play as great a part in our character formation as any formal learning process. Nevertheless, the schools themselves are targeted on formal academic results. They will be judged primarily on rational and objectively verifiable achievement. Whilst good schools will recognise the significant role of pupils' emotional development in this, in the final analysis this is a means to an end, the end goal being recorded success against standard examinations.

So the cortex is exposed to an intense learning process over many years allowing the student to prepare herself for the demands of structured society. So far, so good, but then come the teenage years.

ADOLESCENCE

All parents of a nervous disposition should look away now or at least grab the nearest cushion.

Many of us have 'enjoyed' the opportunity of guiding our children through their adolescence, which we can broadly think of here as the teenage years. Whilst the experience is by no means uniform for all, I am sure we can relate to the typical behaviour changes that surface. Those days when the sons or daughters we once knew appeared to transform into something we could not recognise, when our offspring morphed into another shape, apparently bent on challenging everything we, as parents, stood for and throwing away everything we thought we had taught them. Often this would be accompanied by a distinct change of appearance, not only physically but also in terms of dress sense; personal teenage appearance became a no-go area for the parental mind.

So to help us cope with this potential sea-change in the parent-child relationship it is helpful to understand some of the key drivers of this adolescent behaviour change. The development of puberty is, of course, one of these drivers and is generally understood at a popular level. Seeing your own body change shape and dealing for the first time at a personal physical level with both the excitement and fear of sexuality is itself a challenging experience. And when these personal factors are thrown into the melting pot of the collective school environment it is not surprising that the result we often see is a volatile concoction of youthful energy and expression.

The sudden acceleration of physical and sexual growth itself places emotional demands on the adolescent. It's not easy seeing the girl in the mirror changing so rapidly. Add to this the fact that it is often a time of emotional intensity as new relationships are formed and existing ones challenged. Then, to top it all, she has to cope with the biggest embarrassment of all: the horror of blushing! It's bad enough that there is all this stuff going on inside our bodies, and then comes the added burden of the physical and emotional betrayal of the reddened face, just when she is trying to hold it all together! Blushing is a classic physical symptom of the growing sense of awkwardness of the teenager as she experiments with her new social boundaries and sense of identity. Evolution has done the teenage ego no favours here: all the physical and emotional signs portrayed publically for all to see and judge!

Apart from practical changes to matters like sleep patterns, it is the hormonal changes of the teenage years which really hold the key to their behaviour. Adolescence is nature's way of giving our offspring emotional independence from their parents. From the age of about 12, the hormonal chemistry of the brain will change to foster the teenager's sense of personal identity and to think and feel for herself. It is nature's way of preparing her for the reality that her parents will not be around forever.

As parents, we will of course continue to have an important role in supporting and guiding our children but from this time their brains will become less directly susceptible to our shaping, consciously or otherwise. From the perspective of their own survival it is critical that they become self-dependent rather than parent-dependent. The resultant hormonal surge will encourage them to start seeking out their own identity. Mum and Dad's views are no longer enough. Through life they have navigated the views of friends and enemies alike and now it is time to start making their own mind up. For some this will be a gradual process of discovery and reflection; for others it will involve radical swings in perspective and behaviour.

So, the reassurance for parents who feel they are losing control of their children at this time is that they are meant to! Evolution is at work and the survival of the gene is an irresistible force. We haven't done anything wrong or failed to do something. The fundamental forces in play are beyond our control. Not that this observation will sweeten all the emotional turbulence that can be involved, but it can remind us that our role as parents itself needs to evolve to one where we no longer have the assumed right to control, to one where the relationship becomes one of mentoring and collaboration rather than authority and blind faith. The child that does not challenge her parental barriers is the child that does not find herself. Our job is to maintain the essential protective boundaries as best we can but at the same time to allow the space and opportunity within these boundaries for personal search, exploration and growth.

THE MATURING OF THE PRE-FRONTAL CORTEX: THE 'ADULT' BRAIN

So our hormonal changes have set us up as emerging adults to pursue our own life path and, as part of this, the education system looks to us in our late teens to start to make choices about further education or preferred occupations. From a broad educational and social system perspective this is logical as universities are geared to take us into their institutions at around age 18. Yet there is something of an anomaly here when we consider the level of maturity we have reached to make these decisions.

Young adults will by this age have undergone most of the more radical physical changes triggered by puberty, although they will be handling the emotional effects of this for many years to come. However, from a brain perspective, the next maturity milestone occurs a little later and will be less obvious to the external eye; this comes with the maturing of the pre-frontal cortex at around the age of 24.

The pre-frontal cortex is, as the name suggests, situated at the front of the cortex. Whilst most of the cortex is concerned with data processing and task execution, here is the area where we are able to step back and reflect more fully on our life experience and the meaning we bring to it. It accesses data in wider areas of the brain (cortex, limbic and basal) and integrates this to make broader sense of our lives, including the interaction between ourselves, our external environment, including our interpersonal relationships.

The pre-frontal cortex is the essence of what differentiates us as humans. It is where we make decisions and where we try to see ourselves as others do. Its functions include complex communication, emotional balance, response flexibility, fear moderation, empathy insights, moral evaluation and intuition. It is also the place where we plan, process ideas and anticipate the future on the basis of what has happened in the past. And, perhaps most crucially of all, it is the centre of our self-awareness.

Self-awareness does not always come easily to the growing teenager. Yet, it is critical for us that we develop our sense of self as a platform for ongoing personal development. If we simply react to stimuli in the same repetitive way, we are likely to develop a robotic existence and our opportunity for learning is very limited. This is the region of accumulated life learning where we constantly review our own perception of who we are and how we present ourselves to those around us. It is where we can adopt a bigger picture perspective of how we fit into our environment and how we make sense of it. And a necessary part of the development of the pre-frontal cortex is the search for life meaning.

Understanding our place in the universe is much more than a transactional perspective, much more than understanding the mechanics of the universal system of which we are a part. For us, purpose and emotional value are tightly entwined. It is not enough to be concerned solely with our survival in the universe; we have to pursue true meaning through the emotional context of our experience. This means answering the question 'why?' – a subject we shall return to in greater depth in later chapters.

At the age of 24 we may well have started to ask ourselves some questions about the wider meaning of life, but at the very least we will be engrossed in the pursuit of establishing who we are. We will be starting to firm up our decisions around the type of life role we expect to fulfil and exploring how we share this with those that matter to us. Of course, it is a process that continues throughout our lifetime, sometimes offering us validation of our perspective and other times challenging our assumptions at the very core.

From this tender stage of our emerging maturity we will find ourselves making decisions which will position us, both internally and externally, for how we experience and make sense of our lives. For some this could be a journey of ongoing fine-tuning and continuity of purpose. For others it could be a volatile journey of re-thinks and re-starts. For most it will be a mixture of both, of times when our lives simply make sense, consciously or unconsciously, and other times when we feel lost and challenged at the deepest of personal levels.

SECTION 2:
FURTHER INSIGHTS

Hopefully, the information already outlined has whetted your appetite for more, so there are additional features I would like to share here. These will be helpful in laying the foundation for the discussion we will have in the later stages of this book.

CHAPTER 2.1:

The Basal Region: The Instinctive Brain

I explained earlier that the basal region sits just above the brain stem at the base of the head and is the oldest part of the brain. Its key role is ensuring the survival of the organism. Just like the crocodile, it only does what it needs to and does not overcomplicate life. In behavioural terms, when it acts it does so decisively and swiftly. There is no room for negotiation.

This may sound a little brutal and indeed it is. The essential evolutionary design of the basal brain was sculpted when the environment we faced was itself brutal. No time for niceties when you need all your energy to survive. Yet survive we did, and this piece of machinery deserves our utmost respect for looking after our species through the millennia. We always do well to heed our instincts when we are aware of them; they are not the full story but their purpose is always to keep us safe. I trust the rest of the book will help to explain them further and to place them within the wider context of total human intelligence.

We may think of the basal region of the brain as being the home of our instincts. For everyday purposes it is useful to think of instincts as the genetic programmes we were born with, our DNA, our survival kit of instructions. As we pass through life, we populate these genetic programmes with experiential data, the experience of life. In common conversation we often use the terms instinctive and intuitive interchangeably. For me, the subtle distinction is that whereas we are born with our instincts, intuition only develops after birth and continues to do so throughout our life. It remains connected to our instincts but becomes more refined as we build our catalogue of experience and learning. So a pragmatic definition of intuition may be: instincts + life data = intuition.

Whichever term we prefer to use, the point is that we experience the sensation of intuitive or instinctive response instantaneously. It seems to come from a deeper place and we cannot always explain why we have responded this way. Intuitive responses are indeed linked to the arousal systems that sit in the base of the brain and each of these systems operates without conscious input. They do not wait for logical permission to engage.

These arousal systems are built significantly around four main hormones. These are acetylcholine, noradrenaline, dopamine and serotonin. Noradrenaline is concerned with priming the body to act and acetylcholine to rebalance it afterwards. Dopamine is the hormone of reward and serotonin is the hormone of happiness and attachment. Each of these provides a fundamental influence on our behaviour.

Our instinctive responses are hard to ignore, even though we may not always be clear about where they came from. They have to be invasive because they are trying to keep us alive and to influence us in directions that will be beneficial to our genes, such as security and reproduction. They would hardly work well if we got caught up in emotional distraction or logical trivia and failed to notice an imminent threat. Instinctive reactions can manifest themselves in many ways. It could be reacting to a threat which endangers our lives, such as the noise of an explosion. Or it could be a more subtle trigger, such as meeting someone who reminds us of a person who did us no good in the past.

There are some practical examples that help us recognise when our instincts are at work. Try standing at the glass barrier of an animal enclosure when there is something threatening on the other side. Let's say it's a snake or a tiger. Even though you absolutely know that the glass barrier is secure and reliable, if the animal suddenly attacks the glass in front of you then you will react in fear by recoiling away. Even if you work hard at it and succeed in reducing your response, your eyes will still startle and your heart will still race.

Then there is the example of the mother glancing into a poorly lit room and spotting a snake in the corner. She runs out of the room screaming. Her son then goes in to investigate and sees that it was actually a coiled rope! This does not mean that the mother's instincts were wrong. Hers was the right reaction in the light of the information available to her at the time. The only negative consequence of her perceiving a snake was embarrassment. If it was really a snake and she thought it was a rope the consequences could have been much harsher.

These may be obvious illustrations but our instincts can influence us on a much more subtle level. Take pricing displays in retail. For many years it has remained common practice for most goods on sale in retail to be priced, say, at £3.99 rather than £4. We all recognise that the difference is just 1p, hardly a major factor when considered from a logical standpoint. Yet this is not about logic. Initially it's about triggering the most favourable reaction to the price. And the instinctive brain works quicker than the logical brain, so often our first reaction to the 3 in the sequence has already predisposed us either positively or negatively to how we will view the remaining figures. Instinctively we have seen the first figure and, to some degree, the rest is just detail.

Also consider experiments made with subliminal TV advertising which began in the USA in the late 1950s. By flashing a product image or association at a speed that the conscious brain has no time to register, businesses were able to see a significant impact on their sales success. So, although we could not consciously recall what the image was, our instinctive brain had already registered the image and the process of favourable association had already been triggered. And by favourable association here I mean selling! The visual image had in effect already triggered the response of our autonomic nervous system (ANS) and this sits well beyond the direct control of the logical brain. Such advertising soon became illegal.

CHAPTER 2.2:

The Limbic Region: The Emotional Brain

As was explained earlier, the evolution of the limbic system accelerated in mammals and gave them the capacity for social cooperation and grouping. The limbic and basal regions have been working together long before the neo-cortex started to get in on the act. They are evolutionary soul-mates and much of their interdynamics takes place well beyond the reach of the conscious thinking brain.

When evolution responded to the perceived need to operate in groups, it recognised that this had to be more than just a transactional process. Factors such as loyalty, nurturing and deeper interpersonal understanding had to be fostered at an emotional level. It became therefore not just about recognising the needs of fellow collaborators but also feeling them. The limbic system of the brain is where we feel not only our own emotional state but also where we can recreate the feelings of others.

In the next few pages we will explore further insights associated with the limbic region but first let's look at emotions in more detail. Neuroscientists will typically draw a distinction between emotions and feelings. Although we tend to use the terms synonymously in everyday life, the distinction here is important. We will often talk about feelings and could probably think of hundreds of examples, such as anxiety, frustration, contentment and impatience. For neuroscientists, these are a blend of the basic emotions that underlie them. The neuroscientific community is still not completely agreed on what these basic emotions are but I will share with you here those that now seem to be quoted most frequently.

As a general rule, the lay person thinks of emotions as being either good or bad but in terms of evolutionary purpose such a distinction is inappropriate. Our brains never do anything to intentionally detract from our purpose of survival. So whilst we relate to the experience of these emotions as being either good or bad, in survival terms they all have a critical purpose which we would do well to consider.

Equally important, in identifying and distinguishing between these emotions neuroscience draws only partly on the behaviours we recognise when people are 'being emotional'. A behavioural analysis alone would be too superficial and would not tell us enough about what was going on in the brain and body to trigger these behaviours. So, from a neuroscientific perspective, each of the emotions is separately identifiable as different hormonal states, involving varying neural networks and with differing impacts on the autonomic nervous system. So let's identify these basic emotions.

THE CORE EMOTIONS

In general parlance, there are five emotions we associate as being negative (an unpleasant experience) and these are fear, anger, disgust, sadness and shame. Interestingly, there are only two recognised as being positive emotions, namely love and trust. There is an eighth which we call 'startle', which is the immediate response associated with sudden surprise.

Let's go into each of these. It will be helpful to understand not only what the original evolutionary purpose of each of these emotions was likely to have been, but also to see how these basic emotions have evolved to suit more modern times.

FEAR

Fear can be considered the primary emotion and is specifically geared towards our survival. If the threat is perceived as strong enough it will invade the body's response mechanisms to ensure that all its resources are focused on removal from the threat. In Stone Age times, if we were suddenly confronted by a predator, there was no time for wondering where it came from. We may only have a split second to respond: stay and fight or run like hell! The case for prioritisation of resources was clear and non-negotiable.

Today the fear response operates in much more subtle ways and will be triggered by perceived social threat, loss of status and personal criticism. Now it's less a case of physical withdrawal, instead we have developed a whole array of elaborate threat avoidance behaviours which we demonstrate frequently in social exchanges, ranging from defensiveness to shutting down or intricate verbal exchanges. We may have decided to stay physically present when confronted with social threat but the fear challenge still sits with us at the heart of our emotional and behavioural responses.

ANGER

Anger can be seen as a specific version of the fear response, but whereas fear is at least initially about withdrawal from the threat, anger is focused on confrontation of the threat itself. In anger we mobilise a different set of hormonal responses and neurological networks to enable the targeted outcome of destruction or removal of the threat. Once again, our behaviour has evolved from the Stone

Age response to stand and fight our ground. Although physical confrontation remains one of the options, the modern response will often involve just behavioural and verbal confrontation.

DISGUST

All of us will at some time have experienced the sensation of disgust. It is that feeling of repulsion that causes us to withdraw from a person or situation. It is rarely a considered reaction, more one that seems to act at an instinctive pace and comes very much from within ourselves. The evolutionary purpose here is likely to be withdrawal from a threat of infection. Whereas our fear response is usually triggered by the visual senses (either externally viewed or internally imagined), appearance alone is not reliable. In earlier times we would have had a much more acute sense of smell to warn us of possible dangers of contagious disease or toxic food.

Today, we rely less on smell but the fear of infection has survived, now expressed more as the fear of social contagion. We protect the genes of our social grouping by maintaining distance from those who do not conform sufficiently to our norms.

SADNESS

We all recognise the signs of sadness in others and, indeed, have experienced it for ourselves. Whilst easily recognised, what could possibly be the evolutionary purpose of sadness? After all, there is nothing pleasant about it. The answer is that it is a healing process. Because mammals, including humans, are built as social beings, we feel bonds towards each other. The closer the relationship, the stronger the bond. It is therefore inevitable that we feel a sense of loss when we lose someone with whom we had previously bonded. Sadness is essentially the process of us coming to terms with that loss, acknowledging the gap that has now appeared in our social experience and coping with the process of adjusting to that loss.

So, although unpleasant, sadness is naturally a healthy process whereby the body rebalances to adjust to its new reality. Although success is never guaranteed, dealing with the reality of loss is far better than the ongoing pain of denial. Denial keeps us in an energetic space where the body cannot move on. Mentally an individual might be trying to convince himself that the pain of loss isn't real and that everything is OK but the reality is that the experience of loss is undeniable at a deeper unconscious level. In this scenario, the thinking brain is trying to convince the emotional brain of a supposed state that does not correspond to the energetic reality and is doomed to fail. Acknowledgement of the loss is the only effective starting point for the successful adaptation to change.

SHAME

Now we come to perhaps the least obvious of the basic emotions. Yet, for me, it is a particularly fascinating one. It is doubtful that many mammals experience shame, other than the more advanced primates and only to a very limited level. In fact, for the most part we can consider it a uniquely human emotion, which is not true for the other emotions already explained. So why does the emotion of shame support the survival of our species? Not obvious is it?

The answer lies in understanding the development of social cohesion. We saw earlier that emotional bonding is crucial to the sustainability of social groups. Shame takes this a step further. It is the price of failing to comply with the social groupings' norms, behaviours and values. The threat of shame strikes at the very root of our emotional existence. People who state that they don't care what others think are fooling themselves. They may outwardly pay less regard to the reactions of others than some but nobody can ultimately handle the destructive power of unmitigated shame.

For example, our entire justice system is built on it. Yes, there is the threat of physical imprisonment and even death, but for most the threat of shame is what stops us flouting the rules in the first place. Each of us has inside our head that little voice that is reminding us of the horror of shame if we transgress in the eyes of others. We may deal with it in different ways and the social groups to whom we refer may vary (such as the serial criminal being more concerned about the thoughts of others in his peer group than the judgement of the legal hierarchy) but we all seek the approval of those who matter most to us. The avoidance of shame remains a huge driver in modern human behaviour, albeit we would now recognise this threat more as loss of face and social status. We are intrinsically tuned into our social standing and very sensitive to anything that may threaten it.

So, with all these basic emotions we have seen how they have evolved to manifest themselves in different behavioural patterns that are still demonstrable in modern society. Although now appearing in many different guises, we would do well to try to understand the basic emotions that are in play when we observe or experience social challenge or conflict.

I stated earlier that it was 'interesting' that we recognise five so-called negative emotions and only two 'positive' emotions. On reflection, this makes sense. If we cannot work out how to survive, the motivation of positive emotions is pretty academic!

Let's now turn to what we should perhaps call the 'enjoyable' emotions. Typically these are recognised as happiness and trust.

HAPPINESS

Even the term itself spreads a glimmer of hope on what may otherwise by now be feeling like a very grim emotional landscape. I am sure it is something we can all relate to and find it easy to recognise the signs of happiness in ourselves and others. It may be associated with laughter, fun and generally feeling good in the moment. The other term often used here is 'excitement'. So happiness is a high arousal state, an in-the-moment feeling of enjoyment and vibrancy.

TRUST

Here trust is used in the sense of a deep-rooted contentment, a sense of peace and fulfilment. It is likely to be sustainable and resilient. Whilst happiness is the positive experience of life in the moment it is more likely to be temporary as the high energy level is not sustainable. Trust, however, is a state of calm, where very little energy is consumed and where the emotional benefits are capable of being much longer lasting.

Sometimes we would substitute the word trust for love within the context of a relationship between two people, but it is not just that; it is equally about trusting ourselves. We will experience this in situations where we feel we belong. This is a key consideration when we come to deal with confidence and belief later in the book.

> *"Thousands of candles can be lit from a single candle, and the life of the candle will not be shortened. Happiness never decreases by being shared."*
>
> **– Buddha**

On a deeper level, we may think of love as an extended version of trust. So, whilst happiness is the feeling of falling in love with someone and accompanied by all the surrounding excitement and drama, being in love is an ongoing state of peace and fulfilment. Happiness and trust are often referred to as attachment emotions in that they signify a commitment to another person, belief or cause. In this state we want to step away from our fears and attach to a person or place where our primary feelings are linked more directly to a perceived opportunity to thrive.

ENERGY

I referred briefly in Chapter 1 to the importance of recognising energy as a key medium in our experience of life. I am not limiting this here to our own energetic state but also include the energetic states we share with others. It feels to me that this has been underplayed by many psychological disciplines, particularly in the 20th century.

Frequently, psychology has aimed to explain human emotional states by seeing them as a reflection of our mental state. To a degree this is true, but it is not true to imply that our mental state of mind drives our emotional state. There is a complex interaction constantly going on between body and mind which needs to be explored further.

At this point it is important to remind ourselves that early human communication capability pre-dated language. For many thousands of years humans communicated in the same way that most mammals did: it was more body to body communication than mind to mind. The mental capacities and communication skills we have today were simply not available to the primitive human mind and only really arrived with the accelerated evolution of the neo-cortex.

Instead, successful human cooperation depended entirely on having a mutual sensitivity to our body states, positioning and the basic noises we could make. If we could not talk through language to communicate, we could at least see, hear and sense each other.

The natural communication medium available to humans was energy, or, more precisely, energetic wave forms, which are a fundamental dynamic of the universe of which we are a part. We learnt to communicate through transmitting and receiving of our respective energetic states. Many emotional states were (and are still) universal to all humans and could therefore be shared to achieve collective understanding. Laughter is an obvious example of a primal communication behaviour which allowed the sharing of a universal emotion, that of happiness.

So the way we managed our own energetic state and transmitted that to others would have been a crucial part of our social success or failure. It is not only what we see but also the way it makes us feel: joyous or terrified, anxious or safe?

It is one thing to see somebody taking up a position where he is prepared to fight you but is it just posturing? Is he really prepared to take me on or is he bluffing? Sensing the energetic state of our potential opponent could be far more useful than simply watching his positioning. The limbic area of the brain is the area where we 'feel felt', where we can really tune into the energy of others.

This energetic sensing ability remains with us today. We have all been in situations where we can sense the mood of another person or group before anything is said or overtly displayed. We have all met people who have an energetic impact on us: the confident manner of a successful leader who transmits a feeling of assurance and conviction; the contagious enthusiasm of the extrovert who wants to liven up proceedings; the sad demeanour of the victim who has lost faith and meaning. These are essentially energetic transactions that register first in the body and secondly in the mind. Our bodies are communicating before the conscious mind has yet had a chance to make sense of it. Poker players make a living out of this primal basis of communication and whilst the outward signs of success may be measured in the cards they present, the real inner game to be won is that of energetic intelligence and manipulation. The 'poker face' is as important as the hand they have been dealt.

Paul Ekman has carried out some fascinating research into universal emotions and facial expressions. In his book *Emotions Revealed* he demonstrated that many facial expressions are universal, that is they persist regardless of nationality or culture. There are nuances that are clearly different, such as the Chinese inclination to smile even in the face of adversity or the Indian tendency to shake the head indicating a different meaning to that we would interpret in the West. But it seems that there are a basic set of facial gestures that correspond broadly to the basic emotions that have been described above.

Laughter is a clear example of this. Ekman found a consistency of facial expressions across many cultures, including tribes living very isolated lives in the Amazonian forests. Consider blind people: they also naturally smile as an expression of happiness. Yet it would be difficult to argue that this was a behaviour they had visibly learnt from watching their parents.

Likewise, there is a strong consistency of facial expressions across all cultures related to fear, sadness, anger, disgust and joy. It seems that we are born with a set of genetic expressions that will allow us to start communicating with others well before we have the conscious understanding or language to appreciate cultural nuances. The communication of our most basic universal emotions is a fundamental building block in our ability to bond and survive.

CREATIVITY

The limbic region of the brain is also the source of our creativity. The basal region would have had no real concern with such distraction and the thinking brain is far too rule-bound to go with the necessary flow of the creative process. Remember that the limbic brain existed long before the neo-cortex and operated essentially on sensory data. This meant being tuned into our environment, to the pictures, sounds, tastes, smells and substances that surround us. It also meant being tuned into the energetic wave patterns of our world, to the rhythms of the universe. It is a world in which we naturally reach out to connect and to express and to do so without the help or hindrance of method and language.

Creativity itself is about the flow of natural energy through the associative processes of the brain. Associatively we piece together sensory data to see and feel new patterns in our experience, such as expressing the power or beauty of an internal image through the art of a painting, or the sharing of internal emotions through the rhythmic medium of music.

This process of sensory communication and sharing is the domain of the limbic brain and does not rely at its source on the support of the thinking brain. Yes, we may then introduce language to support the communication process further and this will serve to add clarity. But the inspiration and the essence remains emotional and often the artist does not want to offer objective clarity. Art is the subjective expression of our personalised experience and a medium for emotional sharing.

We will develop this theme further later in the book.

DREAMS

An interesting glimpse into the world of the limbic brain is the way we dream. Sleep is critical in sustaining the ongoing health of our brains, including the consolidation of memory. Part of this process is dreaming. We dream every night and typically our dreams will last two to three minutes. However, we will only be able to recall a dream when we have awoken during it. So most dreams happen and pass us by in terms of awareness and memory recall.

The home of our conscious awareness is the cortex. When we sleep the cortex effectively goes into voluntary standby. It has been working hard all day moderating as best it can the antics of the limbic brain and now needs a well-earned rest. The hormone melatonin floods the brain and helps us to relax and switch off from conscious thought and activity. But the limbic brain never switches off. When we look at the role of the amygdala shortly we will see that it is the radar of the brain, constantly on the look-out for potential threats. The amygdala sits at the front of the limbic brain and there is no room here for standby mode. So, while the cortex is resting, the limbic brain carries on with its natural activity.

If we reflect on our dreams we will normally not be able to make any sense of them. In rational terms, they are likely to be a bundle of stories wrapped in the fanciful, ridiculous and scary. They are essentially visual stories that appear to connect in some nonsensical way random memories from our past and recent experiences. In some cases there may be some recurring themes which reflect an ongoing underlying anxiety or wish, but most of the time they make no logical sense and this is because they are not supposed to. Logic is the concern of the cortex and is of no interest to the limbic brain.

So dreams can be considered a window into the limbic world, one of *experience* reflected in visual episodes linked loosely by an energetic flow.

Curiously we can see some parallels when we have succumbed to the temptation of alcoholic excess (as if!). In this case the chemical effect on the brain takes the cortex into a state of involuntary standby. This can be socially exciting but also dangerous as the moderating influence of the cortex has been minimised. Whereas we are normally inclined to think for a moment before we speak, when we are intoxicated no such filter is in place. If we feel something strongly, which is very likely when we have been drinking, it therefore follows that we will express it – immediately and without the need for deliberation on the consequences that might follow. The next morning may bring with it a feeling of guilt and remorse but it is too late! We profess that 'we didn't mean it', but that of course is not true. At the time we did mean it and regretting it now is only one small step in the journey of personal and social recovery.

THE AMYGDALA

The amygdala consists of a pair of almond-shaped structures which are located roughly behind the eyes. It performs an incredibly complex role which has a profound effect on our experience of life. This includes safety, emotional value and memory.

First and foremost, it is the guardian of our safety. It operates as radar scanning across electromagnetic wave forms and visual imagery to spot anything that might jeopardise our survival. It will examine both external events and our own internal images to identify threat. Equally, in accordance with our more basic mammalian instincts, it will sense the energy of a potential friend or foe to decide if immediate action is required. And to enable it to perform this role effectively it has significant power within the brain.

There is no point in having a safety alarm system that could be slowed down by the machinations of the thinking brain. When the bear comes from behind the bush and is about to tear our head off, it is not a great time for wondering what sort of day he may have had. It is time to act – without analysis and without emotional distraction.

The architecture of the brain means that the amygdala is in a position to call the shots when emergency arises. Its neural connections penetrate all the areas of the brain that are essential to dealing with threat. This includes the basal ganglia which sits at the top of the brain stem and is responsible, amongst other things, for physical movement via the motor neural system. As such the amygdala will trigger an immediate response to threat whether that is withdrawal or confrontation ('flight or fight'). In extreme threat circumstances, being emotional or making sense of the experience is a luxury that will have to wait.

Animal and human reaction to fear is the same. The instant response to an unexpected threat is to freeze. This may only be a second or two but it allows us to focus all of our attention on both localising the threat (working out where the danger is coming from) and on evaluating the level of threat and potential consequences. The amygdala is central to this. Then comes the immediate choice of withdrawal, submission or attack.

We can all relate to our instinctive response to threat in our everyday lives. It should not be difficult to recall experiences when we have been confronted by a sudden threat, for example a car accident or near-miss. In this event we are likely to have had no conscious awareness of a car travelling on the other side of the road towards us and about to lose control. The first thing we are aware of is when out of our peripheral vision we pick up that the car is moving away from the direction of travel we would normally expect and is coming towards us. If the speed of the oncoming vehicle is quick enough the amygdala will take over and trigger a brain reaction which will direct our activity to give us the best chance of survival, in this case taking immediate evasive action. We can feel the rush of adrenalin as the body is primed to react instantaneously; we do what we have to do and hopefully succeed in getting ourselves to a place of safety.

Then comes the aftershock! We can feel our hearts pounding and our glands sweating but initially we may not be able to work out what has just happened. If the threat wasn't too great our 'senses' will return as our normal neural activity and blood flow in the brain resumes, and slowly we will be able to piece together what has just happened. We will effectively re-balance back to normal operation. However, in cases of extreme trauma the recovery process may be much more protracted and in some cases never entirely successful, as we shall discuss more in a later chapter. Nevertheless, the amygdala has done its job: we are still alive.

To be able to protect us in this way, the amygdala takes on a critical role in memory. This is less about conscious memory and more about our memory of previous experiences. It receives signals via the thalamus, which operates like a relay station located at the front of the brain. It then liaises with the hippocampus, which can be thought of as the brain's filing cabinet. It will then match what it perceives in front of it with past memories to identify and evaluate risk. So if what it perceives looks very similar to a previous experience which inflicted harm on the individual, it will immediately trigger the fear response. If the level of threat is marginal, there will be a similar sequence of reaction but the emotional intensity will be less, something we may typically call anxiety or unease.

The response does not end there. The amygdala has the power to sustain our attention to ensure that any lingering threat does not go unnoticed. We know this: anxiety can be triggered in an instant but it usually takes a lot longer for our body sensations to return to normal.

We have uncovered here the role of the amygdala in assessing emotional value. The context of the fear reaction above is one of assessing threat but actually the amygdala has a role in emotional value well beyond this. It attaches an emotional rating to all experiences and is therefore central to our deeply personal experience of life. It will support us to attach either positive or negative emotional value to the people, relationships and environmental factors that surround us. It enables us to feel, to actually experience the sensation of an emotion. It puts the feel factor into both fear and love. The thinking brain may recognise these states but it is the amygdala, working in conjunction with the broader circuitry of the limbic brain, which will translate this into our own personalised experiences. It is, in this sense, the gateway to our emotional being.

INTELLIGENT EMOTIONS

The term 'emotional intelligence' is now a popular reference in cultural literature. Normally this is associated with the ability to pick up and derive meaning from the dynamics of human interaction. It is about understanding interpersonal engagement on much more than just the logical transactional level. It's about not just the words that we exchange but the tone and energy around the total interaction, including facial gestures and body language.

For most people, our brains are incredibly adept at interpreting the gestures of those with whom we engage. Mat Lieberman's book *Social* offers an amazing explanation of the resonance circuitry of the limbic brain, which allows us to mirror and therefore internally experience our own interpretation of what is going on in the other person's brain. It is our own personalised form of mind reading. Links between the limbic brain and the wider intelligence system of the body, especially the heart, then enable us to turn cognition into our own emotional mirroring. This is the fundamental basis of empathy: feeling what the other person is feeling, not just recognising it.

Daniel Goleman has done much to promote the awareness of emotional intelligence, especially on the back of research carried out in the 1960s which demonstrated that EQ (emotional quota) was just as important as IQ (intelligence quota) in predicting the success of university graduates in their forthcoming careers. Yet, even now, emotional competences are rarely measured with any degree of confidence. Nevertheless, I think we need to flip this language and instead talk about intelligent emotions.

The more we explore the sophistication of our emotional system, the more the intelligence of our emotions is revealed. Of course, we are not talking about intellectual intelligence here, which is strictly the domain of the cortex. We are talking about an incredibly sophisticated emotional system which translates environmental and personal data into body and mind responses. Emotions are data that are typically transmitted biochemically and electromagnetically.

The emotional responses of the body are significantly more complex than our thought systems. This is because the degree of brain circuitry and body system integration required is much higher to enable the conversion of an environmental trigger into a body response. This includes the processing of the initial trigger, the comparison with memory, the evaluation of risk, the triggering of the hormonal glands required to prime the body for action, the excitement of the heart and blood circulation system, and the instruction of the central nervous system to instigate appropriate physical movement – and all within a split second!

Unlike thoughts, which can be allowed to wander without causing damage, emotional responses are very targeted on specific outcomes. The targeted outcome of the fear response is safety; for anger it is removal of the threat; for disgust it is withdrawal from infection; for sadness it is healing; and for shame it is social standing and cohesion. Thoughts can meander their way to random conclusions, but emotions are there for a clear purpose and a specific behavioural outcome.

Furthermore, our language is equally deficient when we talk about emotions as being irrational. They are certainly not rational within the context of conscious logical processing, but they are rational within the context of the brain making the best decisions it can, with the information available to it at the time, to suit the best interests of the organism. Looking from the outside, the behaviour of somebody suffering from a phobia or clinical mental condition will seem irrational, but if we could get inside the brain of the individual concerned our perspective would be very different. If we had experienced the same personal experiences or genetic disposition as the person concerned, our action would indeed reflect a very different viewpoint. The brain cannot be programmed to do anything to work against the interest of the individual it serves. It will always try to work out the best course of action. Even in the case of suicide, the brain has concluded that the pain of living outweighs the assumed pain of death. So we need to be very wary when thinking of 'emotional behaviour' as irrational; such thinking is restrictive and unhelpful to true understanding.

MOTIVATION

Additionally, the limbic system of the brain is the source of our motivation.

Let's revert back for a moment to the description of the list of core emotions that were explained earlier. On the negative side we listed fear, anger, disgust, sadness and shame. All of these are an emotional expression of our survival instinct. When a person is in survival mode she is not open to engagement. In survival mode we hang on to what we have, emotionally withdraw and behave in a defensive, territorial manner. Hardly the basis for motivation!

Instead, to motivate somebody, we have to foster a 'thrive' rather than a 'survive' response. Rather than thinking of the 'survive' and 'thrive' responses as different instincts, it probably makes more sense to think of them as opposite ends of the same instinctive continuum. At the negative end of the continuum we see the immediate extreme actions associated with threat avoidance; at the positive end we sense an opportunity to thrive. This instinct to thrive is fundamental to the species' ability to evolve. Survival in the short term may be the top priority, but in the long term it is not enough. If we stand still in evolutionary terms, it is only a matter of time before our species is outmanoeuvred and overtaken by other competitive species. As humans, we are always on the look-out for opportunities to grow and further safeguard the future of our genes.

When the thrive instinct is triggered, the hormonal reaction in the body is to open the individual for attachment. She no longer feels threatened and instead has sensed an opportunity to enhance her existence. She is now prepared to engage, to reach out. She wants to act and to commit to the cause. At this time the hormonal mix in the brain and body fundamentally changes. Instead of the predominance of such defensive hormones as cortisol, we see dopamine, oxytocin and serotonin released. Dopamine mobilises us to focus on reward, that is the opportunity we are sensing. Serotonin is loosely considered to be the happiness hormone and will boost our sense of optimism. Oxytocin is the hormone of engagement and will enhance our desire to commit to relationships and causes.

This is a powerful mix. The thinking brain does not motivate us as such. We may be able to construct thoughts that, in turn, create associations that can trigger the emotional system into a positive response. But the direct route to motivation is emotional engagement. When the emotional gateways open up, our thoughts will follow. This is a theme we will develop much more when we look at human performance in a later chapter.

CHAPTER 2.3:

The Cortex:
The Rational Brain

The cortex is the upper and outer layer of the brain, which we would recognise as the grey folded mass sitting immediately below the upper and side surfaces of the human skull. Whilst my concern here is more with the factors that directly influence human behaviour, it should be remembered that the cortex is responsible for so much more than just what we might broadly consider as thinking.

Structurally, it can be split broadly into four main areas, which are:

-   the temporal lobe, located in the central region of the cortex

-   the occipital lobe, located at the back

-   the parietal lobe, sitting at the top of the cortex, above the temporal lobe

-   the frontal lobe, situated, as the name suggests, at the front

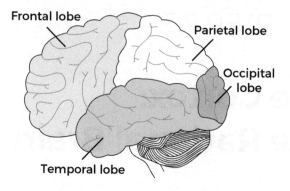

Each lobe has a critical role in supporting our human experience.

The temporal lobe is concerned with long-term visual memory and image recognition, as well as the processing of auditory data. It is also responsible for language recognition.

The occipital lobe is responsible for the processing of visual data.

The parietal lobe is concerned with the integration of sensory data, problem solving, spatial skills, execution and touch.

The frontal lobe is the area of most importance to the purpose of this book. It is the region responsible for rational thought, mental resource allocation, attention, decision making and voluntary movement control.

All mammals have a frontal lobe, but it is the area where the human species has significantly outpaced its evolutionary rivals. The term neocortex, that is 'modern cortex', is a representation of the uniquely human development of the frontal lobe where the evolution of our learning, thinking and language capabilities have so clearly surpassed those of other mammals.

As discussed earlier, the cortex works as a digital network relaying electrical impulses along a series of decision gateways, known as synapses. These synapses create the chemical conditions to enable connectivity across the massive neural capacity of the brain. This is essentially logical circuitry. It is where we lay down the rules (circuits) for our conscious responses and behaviour in life. It is the region of rationality, thinking and deliberate choices, where we establish our very own personal rules for the execution of learnt tasks and behaviour. It's the 'Mr Spock' of our neural capacity.

Within this wider description it is important that we pay particular attention to the pre-frontal cortex as the central player in our awareness of life and in the pursuit of meaning.

THE PRE-FRONTAL CORTEX

The pre-frontal cortex is the centre of our ability to integrate complex intuitive, emotional and rational data. It is the core of our self-awareness and a fundamental navigator in our life experience. To perform such a sophisticated role it is strategically located to have critical connections into all those parts of the brain which can influence our conscious perception and experience of life.

Whilst the amygdala assigns emotional value to a stimulus, the pre-frontal cortex adds language and conscious awareness. Language has been a crucial tool in the refinement of our shared knowledge and ability to communicate. Its impact on the human species in enabling it to clearly surpass other species is self-evident. Language not only supports our ability to express our thoughts but is also a central part of the thinking process itself. It is difficult to imagine how we would be capable of refined thoughts without it.

Whilst the role and value of language is clearly observable to us all, the need for self-awareness and personal meaning is an altogether different phenomenon, sometimes shared and expressed but often hidden away in the deepest recesses of our own internal processing. In creating and sustaining a sense of self, the pre-frontal cortex enables us to maintain a perspective on our own life story, to act as the rudder in the emotional storms that will inevitably befall us.

This self-concept consists of considerations of past, present and future. It is sustained by the generation and explanation of behaviours based on self-image, past memories and the role we expect to play in the future. So, in effect, we are taking the self-concept we have already built in life, examining how it fits with current environmental conditions and projecting how it will need to adapt into the future. To understand this better we need to look further at how memory works in the brain.

MEMORY

Memory is the cornerstone of our personality. It sits at the centre of our view of life and how we have experienced it. It is the immediate base line from which we react to any environmental or interpersonal stimulus. It is constantly evolving to integrate learnings from the present and to project how these may impact us in the future. Yet memory does not sit in one location in the brain. In fact, it is spread across the brain, consisting of brain states which can be triggered by current stimuli. This means that the brain has retained a distributed store of neural connections, each of which evokes a specific memory when required. These billions of brain states cross-connect to offer us the memory of the past that is so vital to how we deal with the present.

Within this, there are two parts of the brain that are critical in the creation and recall of memory: the amygdala and the hippocampus. The amygdala and the hippocampus form a highly sophisticated partnership, whilst at the same time having a clear division of labour. The amygdala deals with emotional memory whilst the hippocampus is concerned with conscious memory.

To understand this better, we need to reflect on how powerful our emotional memories can be when evoked from the past. It may be a personal experience we are feeling now, such as noticing a child at play with his Mum and thinking about how we would have played out similar scenarios when we were young parents. It may be the stimulus of music playing on the radio and evoking the scenes from when we first heard this song and why it meant something special to us. The chances are that we made no conscious effort to commit these earlier experiences to memory but, nonetheless, they have stayed with us and remained part of our own personal emotional reference library that we carry with us wherever we go.

Contrast this with the sheer effort involved in committing conscious learning to memory so that we can get through our school examination. The forced attention we needed to run the subject matter over and over in our minds so that it will hopefully be available to us when the examination question is exposed. Yet the experiences of the school play area are often so much more easily recalled than the subject matter of the classroom. Clearly these are very different experiences and indeed they reflect different processes in the brain.

Again, it is important to remember that from an evolutionary perspective it was critical that we remembered those experiences that were essential to our survival. And it was vital that we were able to do this long before we, as humans, had developed the complex processing of the conscious brain. Consciousness sits in the pre-frontal cortex but the accelerated development of this area of the brain is a very recent development in evolutionary terms. Our memory system therefore inevitably pre-dates conscious choice; survival has demanded that we act decisively when needed, without the luxury of conscious processing.

The first time we saw the bear coming for us was a memory worth keeping in an accessible place so that we could be decisive about our response the next time a similar threat came our way. The amygdala, located at the front of the limbic region of the brain, played the primary role in this. Acting as the brain's radar on the look-out for threats, the amygdala would constantly be matching current events to establish any links with similar events in the past. If a match was established, the appropriate response would be triggered. This meant that the amygdala not only had to have the radar-like sensory data capture abilities but it also had to possess the ability to call on a store of memories. This memory store was created by the brain's emotional system.

This is the fundamental reason why emotional memories stay with us. They are not a product of a conscious decision to capture an event in memory. The need for choice is removed. The amygdala, as explained in the earlier chapter, has the role of attaching emotional value to all our experiences. When the emotional value is judged to be significant, the event will be captured in memory as a brain state (or set of neural connections) that can be re-invoked when the need for recall is triggered.

What an amazing device this pair of almond-shaped structures is: the centre of our emotional experiences and the gatekeeper of our protection from threat. And all of this created and refined long before we became the sophisticated thinking creatures we are now. When we look at pathologies later in the book we will see how emotional memory transpires and sustains in the event of trauma, but for now we will continue to focus on the normal operation of memory.

Let's now turn to the hippocampus, another incredibly complex piece of machinery. Though not a recent evolutionary creation, the role of the hippocampus has increased significantly in humans with the development of our conscious thinking ability.

The hippocampus acts as the crucial partner to the amygdala by integrating memory data from all sources, that is cognitive, temporal, sensory and visual. In this way it creates a memory context located in place and time. It is the filing cabinet of the brain. When the amygdala has spotted an initial match with a previous memory, it is indeed only a very basic comparison. The amygdala acts with speed rather than precision. So when the amygdala comes knocking, the hippocampus responds with the integrated memory data needed to truly evaluate the match and to bring the memory to life and meaning. It produces the relevant 'files' needed to enable us to then make a more informed evaluation of the match the amygdala has spotted.

We can sense this interplay in our everyday lives. In most social situations we will be constantly weighing up the people we are interacting with and responding either positively or defensively depending on our assessment. If the instantaneous emotional assessment of the amygdala is slight we will have time to weigh up the data presented by the hippocampus in a reflective and non-urgent manner. On the other hand, if the emotional stakes are high, the amygdala may override the contribution of the hippocampus and move directly to a behavioural reaction. If the emotional threat or opportunity is imminent, reflection can wait; it's a case of act now and think later.

Therefore, while the amygdala is focusing on emotion, the hippocampus focuses on data. This interplay between the devices also gives us another interesting insight and may help us to understand why conscious memorising is often such hard work. As stated above, we now understand that emotional memories are laid down regardless of conscious choice, so what about conscious memory? What happens when we simply feel the need to remember something to get us through the next everyday challenge?

In this sense, the pre-frontal cortex and hippocampus will collaborate to create conscious memory tracks within the brain. Yet, whilst this collaboration can be impressive, it will always be harder work than the capturing of emotional memories. The inconvenient truth is that unless there is emotional value involved, the amygdala is not interested – and it is the amygdala that calls the shots with unconscious memory. So whilst sustained concentration can indeed create conscious memories, the absence of energetic association will always be an obstacle. This has huge implications for learning. Passive learning without emotional or energetic association will always be harder to achieve. The teacher who can bring his subject alive by stories and pictures which talk to the unconscious levels of the brain will be a teacher who is always remembered.

WORKING MEMORY AND CONSCIOUSNESS

As our thinking ability evolved as humans, what had to come with it was the capacity to hold information in what we now call 'working memory'. We differentiate between long-term and working memory and they are indeed different processes in the brain.

Working memory is where we store information that we need to complete the task in hand. Typically we hold information here for anything from a few seconds to a few minutes. This could be typical language patterns, relevant memories and associations which are triggered by the task to be addressed. Think of it as our working desk. The files and the papers on the desk are needed to complete what we are doing. It therefore operates like a buffer store, holding the required information for a short period of time.

Consider the way we naturally structure our communications without having to stop to think about it. In natural conversation we start a sentence without any conscious awareness of how the sentence may finish. We know what we want to say, so we will just go ahead and say it. We naturally use language structure and tonality to communicate clearly and effectively. The rising or falling of the energy in our conversations will make it clear when we are finishing what we are saying or if we are going on to make another point.

Working memory capacity is limited. It is not designed for holding masses of information. This is why we can only retain a certain amount of information in our heads at one time. Consider any task involving the memorising of numbers. If there is not an identified sequence, such as 1, 2, 3, 4, 5, 6, we will struggle to simultaneously hold too many digits in the required order. Think of game shows on television, when participants are asked to memorise various prizes that may be passing by on a moving belt; we may easily remember the first three in the sequence but then it gets progressively harder as our working memory becomes full and we have to push out old information to make way for new. Whilst there are mental techniques that can be learnt to improve this, built around visualisation and associative thinking, it still demonstrates the point that we have a limited capacity to work with.

So, if working memory is the work desk, long-term memory is the filing cabinet. In brain terms, the hippocampus is the filing cabinet which can give us access to all those life memories that are stored across the neural circuitry of the brain. It is located in such a position as to have this width of neural access and to recall memorised information on demand by triggering the relevant brain states back to life. Of course, we know that despite the wonders of the hippocampus, its performance is not infallible. We know that sometimes we can struggle to recall what we are looking for; other times our memory is uncertain and vague with many gaps to be filled, and we know that our memory performance will deteriorate with age.

We can experience this for ourselves when we are in the flow of a conversation. All is going well until we are asked a surprise question which means we have to stop and recall a longer-term memory before we can answer. We have to pause and give the hippocampus time to retrieve the required memory, which is then brought into the working memory buffer store for immediate use. This retrieved memory will stay in the buffer store for as long as it is activated by the conversation.

Now let's turn again to the subject of consciousness. The importance of consciousness in our evolutionary story should not be underestimated. It is this ability to hold information from many neural sources (visual, sensory, emotional and rational) in the same place for enough time to be able to do something with it that is crucial to our ascendancy as humans.

Most animals have little or no conscious thinking capacity. Even more advanced primates, such as monkeys and gorillas, barely recognise themselves in a mirror. Awareness of self has just not been important in their story of survival; for them it is more important to be highly tuned to their immediate environment and to maximise the value of their sensory data. Thinking could be deemed an indulgence that could cost them their lives. But for humans the ability to hold relevant information in short-term storage, to analyse and evaluate that information and to project the implications into future actions and consequences is fundamental. In this sense, working memory is the home of our consciousness and the host of our concept of 'self'.

It may take a little while to get our heads around this. So, are we saying that animals virtually do no conscious thinking? The normal question would be: how can we know that? We can have some confidence in this knowledge because of the extensive research that has gone into comparing the development of human brains with other mammals and animals. The accelerated evolutionary development of the pre-frontal cortex is unique to humans. We can see no other species with the brain capacity and functionality to perform such conscious thinking tasks.

Even for me, this feels counterintuitive, but it is true. I have been a dog lover for many years and their ability to communicate and connect with humans has consistently impressed me. Surely, when they are dormant they must be thinking about something? Apparently not. Of course, their brains will be constantly processing sensory data – what they see, hear, smell, taste and touch – but they have no concept of future and do not spend time thinking or worrying about it. Dogs, like some other mammals, can be incredibly sensitive to human moods. When, in the past, I have cuddled my dogs, I felt they were giving me just as much back. Their ears would drop and they would be with me entirely and completely, or at least until the next exciting distraction appeared! But this is empathy, an energetic interaction from heart to heart, not from thought to thought. Mammals, like so many animals, can be highly sensitised to our energetic patterns. Horses (and dolphins) are probably the clearest examples of this. Training horses is about sensory and instinctive communication; it's about building trust and communicating confidence. Without these, horse training is impossible and they are too big to be pushed around!

So consciousness can be thought of as awareness of what is in working memory. The emergence of consciousness itself signalled a major transition for the human species from reaction to planned action. We were no longer stuck in the world of stimulus and repetitive response. Now we could survey the information available to us, weigh up the options and make conscious choices about our futures. Conscious choice became a central feature of human growth. In slightly irreverent terms, I have heard the human evolutionary story summed up as us becoming 'emotional lizards with consciousness'!

THE SELF AND INDIVIDUALITY

The pre-frontal cortex and working memory gave us the capacity for self-awareness, the ability to hold information in consciousness and to reflect on our learning from our experiences. This opened up the awareness of our own behaviour and the impact we have on our environment and those around us. Over time, this self-concept has become more and more elaborate and features centrally in psychological disciplines and therapies.

The concept of our own uniqueness remains fundamentally important to us as we intuitively know that there are thoughts, feelings and instincts in our life that belong only to us and cannot be shared by others unless we choose to communicate them. Even then we cannot entirely share the same experience with others; there will always be a corner that is entirely ours.

Our individuality can be understood in terms of the structural design of the brain. Our reactions to our life experiences are the result of the various neurological states that are fired in response to environmental stimuli. In this sense, a state can be thought of as a neural configuration connecting the appropriate pathways for dealing with the stimulus.

The brain appears to have layers of states that underpin our responses, like Meta architecture with specific response states at the top layer producing specific behaviours, and various layers of depth underneath comprising a more generic response pattern that makes us who we are. We are constantly shifting states, but as we move to the deeper levels more personalised patterns become discernible and we start to see the evidence of the specific template that drives each individual brain. Underpinning all of these states sits a core template which represents our own ipseity, the definition of who each of us really is, and encapsulating the essence of our individuality.

CHAPTER 2.4:

The Integrated Brain

Whilst the above explanation of each of the regions of the brain is helpful in understanding their respective specialisms, the reality is that the brain operates essentially as an integrated whole. This can be understood through exploring the examples below.

DECISION MAKING

Humans have been making decisions from the first days of the species, but early decisions were essentially instinctive. The lack of a developed neo-cortex meant that there was no capacity to analyse and reflect, and in these times of high physical environmental threat such thinking could be considered superfluous. Decision making was virtually a reflex reaction to an environmental trigger.

However, as has been discussed, the evolving neo-cortex, and in particular the pre-frontal cortex, brought with it the ability to hold information long enough in working memory to make more considered choices. I am sure you can recognise this today. Nevertheless, the instinctive (basal) part of the brain still plays a significant role in decision making.

Firstly, if the activity of the amygdala spots a match with a previous experience held in memory, it may trigger an instant response. If the match relates to a high perceived threat, the power and speed of the response may be instantaneous and non-negotiable, for example fleeing from a potential predator. On another level, we may experience it as a milder sensation, yet one which feels like it is coming from somewhere deeper in the body. Our reaction may then not be as extreme but it may present us with a discomfort level that we need to try to resolve sooner rather than later. We may describe this as a 'gut reaction'.

You may have come across one of the golden rules of estate agents. Experience has taught them that a potential buyer will decide very quickly whether or not she will buy a house which is up for sale from the point in time that they actually see it. The suggestion is 11 seconds! And I think they are right (give or take a few seconds!). This assumes that the potential purchaser has done some research before actually going to the house, such as internet searching or even just thinking about it (rational data). Then when she gets to the house she discovers two other sources of data: she senses a 'feel' for the house, which probably involves an energetic projection as to how she personally would feel in this environment; and, perhaps most important of all, she gets that first visual impression that will either match or not match with the vision of the house she wants in her head. Such a vision could be explicit and conscious or it could be tucked away in the unconscious mind and only triggered when the stimulus of the new house is seen. Either way, it will be the driving force in the decision-making process.

On the other hand, we may be examining a matter where we have no significant prior experience and so no particular instinctive or associative response is triggered. In this case we are looking at a more rational decision-making process. Essentially there are typically three steps to this process: thinking, feeling and then knowing.

Firstly, we can consider the facts or information available to us in a strictly rational and logical space, the domain of the cortex. We can analyse the evidence and draw a logical conclusion. This may essentially be all that is needed when we are dealing with 'cold facts' or mathematical equations.

However, in the vast majority of problems we encounter there will be a second phase, that of the energetic response. This will take place when the situation we are trying to address triggers an associative memory which results in an emotional response within us. This could be an emotional attachment to something much more subtle, an association tucked away in the limbic system. If the logical analysis and the energetic association match, we are in a place to make an authentic decision and act on it. However, if there is incongruence between logic and emotion we will struggle to resolve the issue. The rational and emotional systems of the brain are working against each other and we will 'spin' between the two, sustaining a feeling of uncertainty and lack of conviction.

Consider those situations where you have just met somebody for the first time. It may be an interview. The candidate is saying all the right things and apparently ticking all the boxes. Yet you have a nagging doubt that makes you wonder if the candidate is authentic. It may be a gut feeling or an association triggered by their body language. Unconsciously it may be an associative memory that is matching the candidate with a previous person in your life who turned out not to be who he said he was (unluckily for the candidate). You are the only person who can resolve the dilemma. Do you go with logic or feeling? In these circumstances you are experiencing the natural tensions of the brain and whichever way you decide will be a risk. If you are feeling this you are not ready to decide and you should consider carefully what further information (internal or external) you need to resolve the matter. This feeling is very different from the natural flow and congruence of an issue that has been thought through, energetically explored and naturally decided.

The phases are not as distinct as it may appear here. There will be a lot of parallel processing but nevertheless the overall pattern is from thinking to feeling to knowing. We 'know' when we have the right answer (at least the right answer for us). It works like a combination lock to the decision-making security safe. We have to discover the combination numbers that unlock firstly the logical key, secondly the emotional key and then the security combination lock clicks into position to open the safe door to knowing. But don't be fooled. It is very rare for us to make truly objective decisions. Science will do all it can to take subjectivity out of the research and analysis process, but for most of us in everyday life our decisions are steered by our emotions and our experience. Our disposition will significantly colour our view of the data. We will decide what is right for us. **The best decisions are made in the quiet place of personal conviction.**

LEFT AND RIGHT BRAIN

To date there seems to have been much popular discussion about the differences between the left and right sides of the human brain. However, to avoid being overly simplistic, I feel that these left and right side distinctions are better understood within the wider context of the triune brain.

As a general rule, we can think of the left side as being the more rational side of the brain, whereas the right side is more emotional. In terms which are more relevant for this book, the essential insight is the neural connectivity between the right side of the cortex and the limbic system is more intense and therefore more tuned into our internal emotional state. For the same reasons, the right side is more creative, contextual and intuitive. The left side is more cognitive, detailed and concerned with targeted processing activity, typically more interested with the objective and external world than what goes on within.

The neurological transmission links that control the physical movement of the body are reversed in the sense that the right side of the brain controls the left side of the body and the left side of the brain controls the right side of the body. We see this when people suffer strokes. If the brain has been damaged on the right side it is the left side of the body that will struggle to recover normal movement.

When it comes to the eyes it gives us an interesting insight into the authenticity of human beings. The right side of the brain controls the left eye and it therefore follows that the left eye will be the greater testimony to personal integrity. A bright, open and welcoming eye can offer us some assurance. A dark, partly closed and 'dead' eye should cause us concern. On the other hand, the right eye, being controlled by the left brain, will give away few of these sensitive signals and will remain rationally attuned to the world of the external environment. Check it out the next time you are not sure if you can trust someone. What is his left eye telling you?

Similarly, we naturally offer our right hand as a handshake, a gesture prompted by the left side of the brain to reach out into the external environment. On the other hand, there is anecdotal evidence that left-handed people are in general more creative than their right-handed counterparts − evidence of the deeper inner connectivity and associative capability of the right side of the brain?

And what about babies? As far as I have seen, and this is clearly anecdotal, babies are far more inclined to suck their left thumbs than their right thumbs. Is this evidence of the soothing connection with the right side of our brains?

GENDER DIFFERENCES

Building on this we can have a quick look at the apparent differences between male and female brains. There are some reliable rules of thumb but they have to be treated with caution. When I talk about gender differences below they are not black and white. We are only talking here about likely tendencies and the degree of overlap between men and women is significant. It may indeed be more helpful to talk about the typical features of 'male brains' and 'female brains' rather than men and women; there are many women displaying the behaviour of 'male brains' and many men displaying features of 'female brains'. Of course, this is an area where we occasionally need to tread very carefully although it usually makes for great light conversation over dinner!

So, simplistically, at the behavioural level we can recognise male behaviour as typically being more targeted and narrower in focus, a legacy from Stone Age times when family survival depended on the male's ability to go out and track his prey. Men have therefore generally developed stronger spatial abilities. For the female, however, biology had determined that her fundamental role was that of looking after the children. So, from the start she developed the talents of nurturing and sensitivity to her immediate environment. Her protective role also included maintaining the safety of the 'nest'. She was therefore closely attuned to the threat of spiders, snakes and any other predator that could sneak into the family home.

These distinctions remain with us today. Men's eyesight is typically stronger at the centre of their vision than women's. This reflects the requirement for male hunters to stay focused when hunting and to be fixed on the movements of their targeted prey. Women tend to have better fields of vision, which was valuable in being able to scan their immediate environments. Nowadays, the distinction might be less important.

Have you ever come across the domestic scenario when Dad has asked Mum where he can find the mayo in the fridge? Mum explains that it is right in front of him but when Dad goes to the fridge he really cannot see it. After some further interchange, Mum gets up and goes to the fridge and immediately points to the mayo! Dad is totally confounded and Mum is equally frustrated.

The truth is that Dad's vision operates like the beam from a torch. Had he shone the beam in the right place, he would have spotted the mayo, and if the mayo had tried to move away from him, he would have been able to work out the speed and angle of its movement and intercepted the runaway before it could do any damage to any other item in the fridge! Mum's vision, on the other hand, operates just like the light coming on when the fridge door opens. She is much better equipped to take a panoramic view and survey the fridge for its contents, even the corners!

Likewise, Dad needs to be very careful if he should notice an attractive female when walking down the street with Mum. Dad does not have the field of vision to have a second glance without turning his head. If he does so, he is likely to get noticed by Mum and any attempt to plead for his innocence is likely to fall on stony ground. Having admonished her shameful counterpart, Mum is now free to continue the walk, knowing she has the visual field to enjoy all that the male species can offer aesthetically without the labour of turning her head!

I recall digging myself into a hole when I tried to explain the concept of male and female brains to my daughter, Natasha, when she was at the tender age of 12. I had just read the Alan and Barbara Pease book *Why Men Don't Listen and Women Can't Read Maps* and took her through a lovely questionnaire the authors had put together to help the reader ascertain how male or female their brain was. When I had taken Natasha through the questions, we totalled her score and she scored quite clearly into the male area.

I realised that the conversation was not going to plan when her mood started to change to one of growing alarm and anxiety. So was I saying she was manly? That she was going to grow up looking unattractive and sexually confused? That the sensitivities of being female would pass her by? You get the drift!

It took some time to convince her that this was nothing to do with the way she would physically develop and grow and that her female attractiveness remained assured. I was simply trying to explain that her thinking style and behaviour was likely to be more male-like in areas such as targeted activity and focus (desperately trying to draw on the positives). I think I got there in the end but I learnt a lesson that day: male or female brain, they need to be treated with due care and attention. Ironically, as we were on holiday, we then went for a game of archery and she beat me! No clearer example of a targeted brain!

Of course, these are flippant anecdotes but there is a serious side to this matter. When we look into the brain itself, there is a bridge running along the central base of the cortex which enables connectivity between the two hemispheres; this is called the corpus callosum.

A closer examination of the corpus callosum shows that there are more interconnections between the hemispheres of the brain in females than there are in males. This supports the popular view of women being more competent at multi-tasking than men. It appears that the female brain has more capacity for parallel processing of tasks. An MRI scan would show many areas of the brain lighting up at the same time. In male brains, however, neural activity is more likely to be concentrated within particular areas. This may result in behaviour which is seen to be targeted or driven. So, keeping this part of the discussion on a generalised level, the average female is more likely to be able to multi-task better than the average male. On the other hand, the average male brain is likely to be more focused and less prone to distraction and changes of mind. Oh dear, I can feel myself digging that hole again!

LEARNING AND PERSONAL CHANGE

"We must always change, renew, rejuvenate ourselves; otherwise, we harden."

– Goethe

When we looked at memory earlier we discovered that learning is more effective when it is associated with an energetic experience. In other words, we are more likely to remember something that is important to us. When the emotions are triggered, the amygdala will support the creation of accessible memory in the brain. Without energy, we are left to force the learning process by repetition and attentive diligence, an arduous and painstaking task.

This is not limited to the subject matter we are dealing with; it also applies to the person or event that has the potential to bring the moment alive. We easily remember good storytellers because they engage our limbic system. The pictures, rhythm and flow of the story captivates us without asking too much of our cognitive concentration. We are with them because we want to be. Storytelling has always been a central part of the skill-set of the accomplished orator.

There is another insight which is especially relevant for teaching purposes. We now know that the brain will learn more effectively when it expects to have to teach. This is another insight into active versus passive learning. When we try to learn passively, we struggle to create a learning context in which we will put the learning to good use. Where we can create an internal picture it acts as an emotional rehearsal, a visual anchor on which we can ground our learning.

The student who is simply learning for learning's sake will need all his powers of concentration to succeed in the task. On the other hand, the student who knows he will shortly be asked to pass on his learning to other students will create a visual scenario in the brain where he can see himself having to perform the required teaching task. He is effectively projecting himself forward into this anticipated challenge; by doing so he is creating purpose and context for his learning, enabling him to focus his energy and concentration accordingly.

So, we can be confident that energetic association can be vital to learning but what about the deeper challenge of personal change? It is one thing to be asked to recall an event or technique; it is something entirely different to be asked to change our behaviour. Of course, we can all comply in the short term with an instruction to behave in a certain way, such as from our boss or teacher, but what if we are being asked to modify our ongoing behaviour to the extent that we are seen to have personally changed our approach or style?

This is, of course, the essence of coaching and, possibly, mentoring. Rather than delving into coaching techniques here I want to stick with the mindset of the individual who wants to change, whether it is through external encouragement or through personal desire. The key is that **there can be no sustainable personal change without emotional access.**

Neuroscience has shown us that it takes about 80 milliseconds to register an emotion in the brain, compared with 250 milliseconds to register a thought. Emotions are faster and stronger and have the power to create new neural pathways. Thoughts, on the other hand, are likely to simply activate the pathways that already exist. Why would the brain waste energy when it already has the machinery to carry out a cognitive task? This is exactly why energy is needed to have the potential to lay down new pathways or to divert existing ones to achieve a different result. Thinking alone uses what we already have; the energy of emotions brings with it the potential for sustainable personal change.

This helps us to understand why personal change is so difficult and especially without support from others. To step outside of ourselves entirely and look back in on who we are is impossible: we will always look through the internal filters created by our own life experience. Cognitive insight alone will not be enough. Simple reflection might be intriguing but it needs to be accompanied by authentic emotional access to the deeper parts of who we are.

The accomplished coach will help us to look back in on ourselves by sharing an external perspective. She will support us to evaluate if change is needed and, if so, what type of change is likely to be best suited to us. This can be a supportive, if challenging, experience and will depend significantly on the trust built between coach and coachee. Even then, the coach cannot do it for us; personal change rests entirely in our own grasp.

On the other hand, sometimes life itself will confront us with the necessity for change. We may not have sought it and we may be ticking along nicely in our own private way, when BANG! life changes the rules! We lose our job, or we lose someone close to us in a tragic accident, or we are diagnosed with a life-threatening illness. Suddenly the old rules don't work anymore. We have to re-adjust and re-create ourselves to cope with the new environment we face. Triggering emotion is not the challenge here, we are swamped with it. Now the challenge is channelling it rather than being swept away.

Fortunately, most of the time in our lives the personal changes we aspire to are incremental and brought about by our own reaction to the way we are experiencing life at the time. We may talk about 'transformational change' but is this really the case within the context of all of the life lessons we have experienced so far?

Nevertheless, how can we use our brains to undertake a level of voluntary change that we feel would make our lives that bit more enjoyable, peaceful and successful? This is where we need to go back to the pre-frontal cortex and working memory.

I have said quite categorically that reflection alone is not enough to trigger sustainable personal change, yet it may be the starting point. We cannot think our way through personal change but we can get our thoughts and feelings working together to give us a better chance. Earlier I explained working memory and how this serves as a buffer store holding key information in instantaneous access for a limited period of time. This buffer indeed gives us a reflective capacity before we consciously choose to act. The pre-frontal cortex is also the home of our concept of self. Combining the two gives us an enriched capacity to think about who we are, and whether or not the way we are living life now is the best way for us to progress.

Our challenge is therefore getting the right blend of cognitive, emotional and intuitive data into working memory so that we can further examine the totality of who we are. The pre-frontal cortex plays a central role in this because it has neural access to all these layers of the brain. We need the intelligence of emotions to understand where our energy is now; we need the deeper intuitive intelligence that has accompanied us through life to act as testimony to our history; and we need clarity of thought to help us create a pathway for our future.

SLEEP

Before leaving this section of the book, it would be useful to have a look at sleep. Sleep is of fundamental importance to the health of the brain. The benefit I am sure we can most easily attest to is its role in energy restoration. We have all experienced the reinvigorating benefits of a good night's sleep, as well as the draining effect of losing out on sleep. The brain has been working hard all day and needs its rest at night.

The primary sleep hormone is melatonin. When we give in to the strains of the day, as we put our heads on the pillow, the brain will flood with melatonin, which has the effect of relaxing the brain and reducing neural activity. Melatonin will support the synchronisation of necessary physiological activity throughout the night, including blood pressure, metabolism and body temperature. This is done through a pattern of activity known as the circadian rhythm.

The circadian rhythm is in effect our 'body clock' and will guide us through the rise and fall of our natural body rhythms. At night we typically go through sleep cycles of about 90 minutes to two hours each. In each of these we drop through the stages from light sleeping into deep sleeping including the dream state, known as the REM (rapid eye movement) stage. All of this is critical to the conservation of energy.

At the same time, sleep for the brain is a time of memory consolidation when some synaptic connections are reinforced and others are weakened. In effect it is evaluating the data that we need to keep and that we don't really need.

Furthermore, sleep is critical as the process by which the brain maintains its own hygiene. Blood capillaries throughout the brain are very active during the day as they serve to support brain cells with the necessary oxygen and nutrients to enable them to function. Each brain cell produces waste and at night time these capillaries transform their activity to absorb and clear this waste. Because neural activity is slowed during sleep so is the demand on blood supply, therefore blood capillaries have spare capacity which they use to transport away the brain's waste. A clean brain will support neural optimisation. On the other hand, the build-up of wastage would seriously hamper synaptic connectivity and reduce brain performance.

CHAPTER 2.5:

The Wider Human Intelligence System

FIVE BRAINS!

So far we have concentrated primarily on the brain but this alone is not enough. When we seek an understanding of human intelligence we need to also consider the roles of other critical organs in the wider human system. Intelligence does not just sit in our heads, it is spread throughout our bodies.

Any theory which is built on the premise that our brains call the shots and the rest of the body follows is fundamentally flawed. I recall being struck by a conversation I had with a senior neurological consultant some years ago when he stopped me in my tracks by explaining to me that each of us has more than one brain – in fact we have five! After checking what he was drinking, and being reassured by the fact that it was just water, the conversation continued.

Of course, when we refer in common language to the brain, we are referring to the one in our head. More precisely, this is the cranial brain, but there are other 'mini-brains' which together form the vast neurological network of our bodies. They are referred to as mini-brains because they have their own neurological systems which allow them to operate with a level of independence from the rest of the intelligence system. Two of these are less important for the purposes of this book; these are situated in the throat area and are responsible respectively for blood circulation and respiration. However, the other two cannot be ignored; they are the heart and the gut.

THE HEART

"The brain gives the heart its sight.
The heart gives the brain its vision."

– Rob Kall

For many years the importance of the heart in the human intelligence system has been significantly underrepresented. In neurological terms, the heart houses the cardiac brain and this performs a critical role in influencing how we feel, behave and perform. The cardiac brain consists of about 100,000 neurons, a figure which appears to pale into insignificance compared with the 90 billion neurons in the cranial brain. Yet, there are two significant factors that belie such a superficial comparison.

Firstly, the reach of the neural fibres extending from the heart travels right up into the brain and creates vital connectivity to the limbic and basal systems. This forms a substantial part of the system responsible for our unconscious reactions to environmental stimuli. So, whilst the number of neurons may not appear large, their role and influence is what really counts. In fact, when we examine the neural activity passing through the vagus nerve, which is the main nerve connecting the brain and the heart, we can see that there are more instructions passing from the heart to the brain than vice-versa. The days of thinking of the neurological relationship between heart and brain as slave and master are now totally discredited. The relationship is one of interdependent partnership: they need each other.

Secondly, the heart's functions extend well beyond that of neural connectivity. It also functions biophysically, biochemically and electromagnetically. In biophysical terms, the sequence of the firing of the chambers of the heart enables it to operate as a pump to create pressure waves which will force the circulation of blood around the body. Blood carries oxygen and other vital nutrients which are essential fuel to sustain every cell in our bodies. In this sense the heart has an extent of direct access that the cranial brain does not. The heart therefore has unique potential to interact with every aspect of our body experience.

Biochemically, the heart creates and releases critical hormones, known as peptides, into the bloodstream, directly impacting areas such as behavioural responses. Earlier in this book we have discussed instinctive reactions to triggers such as fear or associative memories. We have discovered that these reactions can be triggered quicker than our conscious awareness allows. The biochemical function of the heart is a key part of this unconscious responsiveness, a subject we will develop further later.

In terms of energy supply, the heart can be considered the powerhouse of the human body. It generates approximately 50 times the electrical output of the brain, supplying more than 2.5 watts of power. It is the body's main oscillator and generates an electromagnetic signal which is at least 1,000 times greater than that of the brain. Its electrical signal is distributed to every cell in our body. This electrical activity creates waveforms which 'communicate' with every cell through intelligence encoded in electromagnetic form. This is the energetic domain of our existence, where we connect both internally and with the external world.

These energetic transactions take place unconsciously and operate at a speed which is quicker than the rational brain. From an evolutionary perspective, this makes absolute sense. We need to remind ourselves that these capabilities existed long before we developed language and self-awareness. In the early years of the development of the human species we had very limited ability to respond to the world through conscious thought, and so our very survival depended on our senses and their ability to respond immediately to our environment. This is why, even today, the heart gets there before the rational brain. By the time the pre-frontal cortex is engaged, the heart has already started responding to the sensory data it has received. We may describe this as a 'feel' for something and the sensation will precede any attempt to rationalise and make sense of it. This has significant implications for areas like stress, on the one hand, and confidence at the other end of the spectrum. We will return to this in later chapters.

The limbic region of the brain is tuned to pick up on energetic variations and in this way operates in analogue mode, which means it is state sensitive. The cortex works primarily in digital mode, which means its circuitry is built on the basis of neural decision points (synapses) which define the flow of neural activity. The cortex depends on the limbic system to bring emotional and sensing data to the table, and the heart is central to this intelligence.

Furthermore, the heart directly influences creativity and bigger picture thinking. It seems that the electromagnetic domain opens up a wider connective capability which allows the brain to 'think' more widely (access wider reaches of its network), rather than being caught in the trenches of established neural circuitry (conditioned thinking). This is why energy is such a key aspect of creativity. Creativity operates in energetic flow; it cannot be captured in logical rules or structural boxes. Energy does not 'do' rules. Creativity is, by its very nature, the ability to free ourselves of our established thought processes (which sit in the cortex) and link more associatively across the wider spectrum of the brain. The connection between the limbic system and the heart are central to this.

So, whether we are talking neurologically or across the broader functional purpose of the heart, we need to understand and respect its role in providing human intelligence and in influencing our experience of life.

THE GUT

The 'third brain' is located in our gut and is called the enteric system. It is a system that we as yet know so little about, but the evidence is increasing that it plays a significant role in our instinctive intelligence.

The enteric brain consists of about 100 million neurons and has important connections into the basal area of the brain. We often use the term 'gut feeling' and here we are uncovering some of the science which lies behind it. When we experience this, it seems to come from a deeper place within us, broadly associated with the location of our gut. Although we may use the word feel, denoting a physical sensation we experience, it is really better described as an instinct. It is intuitive rather than logical and it comes across as a hunch, a feeling we cannot easily explain in rational terms. Yet it is often compelling, an insight we do not easily set aside.

These impulses are typically triggered by memory and the intuitive processes that sit at the unconscious level. We may have an instinctive association with an environmental stimulus which is triggered into consciousness so that we become aware of it apparently out of the blue. This is associated with both the energetic sensitivity and the neural function of the gut.

The gut also has a key role in producing hormones, which themselves will directly influence our behaviour. These include serotonin, dopamine, oxytocin and cortisol. Ninety per cent of the body's serotonin is produced in the gut, serotonin being the 'happiness hormone'. Dopamine is the hormone associated with reward; it supports the targeting of our behaviour on perceived opportunities. Oxytocin is the hormone of attachment and trust and critical to the bonding of relationships. Cortisol is often called the stress hormone; its function is to fight infection in the body but in excess it causes feelings of anxiety and stress. The mix of these hormones is fundamental to our emotional experience of life and it is the gut which sits at the centre of this.

So we are rapidly discovering a deeper understanding of the total human intelligence system, with the brain, heart and gut being the central players. We can also see that so much of this activity is triggered at the unconscious level, with our conscious awareness only coming on board when the activity is already underway. Emotions are fundamental neurological states (connectivity patterns) and body responses triggered by associative memory and form the essential ingredients of our lives. In this sense, at least, rational thought is simply the icing on the cake.

Consider just how amazing this total system is and it operates in milliseconds! It is a system of highly sophisticated process and machinery delivering a split-second response to a fear-registering stimulus, absorbing data, recalling memory, assessing options, predicting consequences, decision making and execution. Sensory inputs trigger the emotional system, which in turn triggers automatic hormonal and behavioural responses. The experience is then represented in working memory by the pre-frontal cortex to maintain awareness of the issue and to register learning insights that may be valuable for dealing with future similar events.

The cranial brain cannot operate in isolation from the body; it depends on the rest of the intelligence system to provide the required bio-feedback to operate in real time and to support and respond to the situation being faced. An amazing complexity of data and responses orchestrated at breakneck speed and built with the primary purpose of keeping us alive.

SECTION 3:
THE HUMAN
ENVIRONMENT

CHAPTER 3.1:

Relationships

"Where the heart lies, let the brain lie also."

– Robert Browning

THE EARLY YEARS

Until now, this book has focused mainly on the neuroscientific principles which underpin our existence as human beings. Now we move further into the more interpretive space and look at some of the everyday features of our lives and reflect on how they play out these principles. Examining the role of relationships is a great place to start as they play a huge part in defining who we are.

Our emotional experiences have a major impact on the development of our brains. Earlier in the book we looked at how our relationship with our mother directly influences the early development of the brain in the womb even before we are born. A relaxed mother will have a calm heart rhythm and this will transmit to the baby's heart in the womb offering comfort and security. On the other hand, if the mother is tense and anxious, the baby will already start preparing for a more hostile world.

When the baby arrives, she will immediately depend on her mother and father for her survival. This starts with the baby crying to attract attention. It is highly unlikely that she is actually upset in the way that we would normally recognise it. The baby is just following her genetic instincts that tell her to cry at a pitch that parents cannot ignore. Of course, if she is ignored the level and intensity of the crying is likely to increase but if being ignored continues she will eventually stop. This will certainly resonate with parents of young babies. Crying is the most difficult sound to ignore: it is pitched at a level that seems to strike right into our hearts. If we run to the baby every time she starts to cry we know we are creating an expectation that she will expect to continue. On the other hand, if we respond too infrequently we are left to battle with personal feelings of guilt and anxiety.

For most of us it is a case of finding the right balance and, hopefully, over the early months we will establish a healthy pattern of response and expectation. However, for babies robbed of such responsiveness the picture is much darker. When babies are faced with a world that does not respond, their brain will stop developing.

Sadly, this was demonstrated so clearly in the cases of the Romanian orphans that hit the media in the 1980s and 1990s. Young infants, deprived of adult interaction and stimulation, simply stagnated in their orphanages. The infant brain's main source of learning and development is the emotional response they get from their care givers: no response equals no development. The orphans' behaviour was therefore typically withdrawn and disinterested. They existed in body but 'the lights were out'.

Experience since then has shown that those infants who were 'rescued' within the first two years of their lives generally went on to fully recover from their very slow start in life, whereas those who were older saw the developmental deficit stay with them permanently. As so often in neuroscience, we learn from the circumstances when brain development does not go to plan. In this case it simply amplifies just how important our role as parents is in those early years.

But what about the parents themselves? Earlier we covered the hormonal changes that both mother and father will be experiencing. The intensity of connection for most new parents is undeniable. I certainly recall the birth of all three of my children with deep affection. It's that first feeling of unconditional love. Love between couples is, of course, equally important but the biology of the love for your child feels different. People in relationships have to go through all the normal social, emotional and rational routines to find and fall in love with each other. With your new child, there is no choice; your hormones and genetics have already conspired to make the choice for you. You are smitten and the impact is immediate.

More recently, I have become a grandfather and the experience has taken me right back to those same emotional connections. It amazes me how a child aged just two years can have such a huge impact by the most basic of emotional transactions: the power of the greeting smile, the warmth of the tender hug or the sheer exhilaration and laughter of tackling a new task or challenge. What an incredible demonstration of the power of human connection, stripped away from the complexities and rational distractions of adulthood; the child without talking to our child within.

PARENTAL INFLUENCES

I think any reader of this book would do well to reflect at this point on the respective influences of his/her parents. For my part, as I look back on life, I can see those features I have inherited respectively from my Mum and Dad. In fact, I can only do this through memory of the key parental behaviours that I can still access.

My Mum was stoic, the typical product of a woman raised in the mining valleys of South Wales. She personified the culture of the area: uncompromising, but capable of deep affection and commitment, and armed with a gorgeous and quick wit that could light up any room. She had many personal challenges to cope with in her life, including the death of her brother at the age of 24 through a collapse at the local mine; her first son contracting meningitis at the age of just a few months and leaving him permanently deaf; and the hollow absences of her husband spending large periods of time away from home during the Second World War, sometimes missing without any word of his safety for many months at a time.

My Dad was gentle, a true friend who would always resort to reason and sensitivity before aggression. If he ever had any aggressive tendencies they were crushed out of him in the war time, when he spent his time in the Royal Navy. He saw a great deal of conflict and the conversations I had with him about this as a child will stay with me forever. He held no bitterness and no anger, just a deep sense of sadness at how destructive men could be to one another. Yet, this was always balanced by a huge sense of pride in those he fought with, the depth of camaraderie shared by those whose lives depended on each other. He lost many close friends in the war and always felt incredibly grateful to have survived its horrors himself.

So, in myself I recognise both the strength of character and the single-mindedness I believe I inherited from my Mum, and some of the gentler human touches and sense of gratitude I was taught by my Dad. I recognise the weaknesses also, but it would take another book to cover those. Nevertheless, I was blessed in that I always felt loved, a love that has served as my bedrock as I have taken on the ups and downs of life.

And so can we all reflect on how much our parents have influenced us. I have to chuckle when I frequently hear people say things like 'Oh no, I can see myself turning into my mother!' They may not always be a physical part of our everyday lives now, but make no mistake, they have had a significant say on the development of our brains.

SOCIAL INTERACTION

As stated earlier, our brains are wired for social interaction, especially the limbic region. We need other people in our lives, not only for the practicalities but also for the emotional and rational feedback we get from relationships. Our view of ourselves is not a static state, it is something that we are constantly sculpting throughout our lives. We seek the response of others to help us understand if we are in the right place and creating the right impact or if we are creating impressions and consequences we do not seek. This experiential and emotional data is vital to sustain us or to guide us along a different path. Even hermits need relationships, although it is more likely to be with their pets. Solitary monks would not survive without their relationship with their 'God'.

We are all designed to look for social meaning and we do this through sensing and reflecting on our relationships. These will range from long-lasting relationships to those fleeting interactions we experience on a day to day basis. The impact we have on each other is significant, right from the first encounter. We will sense each other's energy even before the rational brain has become involved.

When we walk into a shop and are greeted by a welcoming smile and engaged eyes, there is every chance that we will respond in a similar way; if we are greeted with disinterest we will struggle to offer anything back. This is known as energetic priming and has been part of us since long before the neo-cortex became a big player.

Likewise, we have resonance circuitry located within the limbic system and this helps us to feel what the other person is feeling.

The circuitry operates energetically and picks up signals from our companion. These signals are converted into our own experience in our own brain and heart so that we can, in effect, mirror the experience of others. This is the essence of empathy and mutual understanding.

Additionally, we have a dedicated area of the brain devoted exclusively to facial recognition. We will focus initially on the faces of people we meet to look for instant clues as to whether they can be trusted or if we should be wary of them. This will happen instantaneously: we start processing facial recognition data within 33 milliseconds of the encounter.

All of these capabilities are testimony to the power of relationships, to the fundamental roles they have played in our development to date, and to the continuing emotional value we place on them today. In fact, when we examine the brain in the process of relationship bonding we can see that it opens up. The attachment emotions we discussed earlier are triggered and the biochemistry of the brain changes with the influx of hormones such as oxytocin and serotonin. Oxytocin, in particular, is the hormone of engagement. It opens our brain up to new energy and influences; it causes our eyes to sparkle as we seek a new relationship adventure. Hopefully we can all recall times when we have met someone we were attracted to and there is that poignant moment when our eyes meet, and we feel a visceral sense of connection; we are drawn in by the deep allure and our eyes become the windows to the soul. Actually, it's probably the oxytocin!

This is in stark contrast to the hormones associated with survival emotions, especially cortisol. When we sense danger, including social threat, our brains consolidate activity into the areas most important for survival. We concentrate on our own needs, become emotionally territorial and pull up the drawbridge. We become a narrow version of ourselves. Yet, when we bond into a trusted relationship, the chemistry and awareness of our own boundaries dissipates and we are available to become part of a bigger whole, when two become one! (There you go, I can do romantic!)

This is the basis for loving relationships. Our brains are open to profound engagement with the person we love. Even our sense of self-identity can become merged with the identity of us both. In a healthy relationship we will search out mutual interdependence when both are critical to the success of the whole. In fact, human nature demands a level of felt equality if the relationship is to be emotionally sustainable. To enjoy ongoing happiness as a loving relationship there needs to be a clear and shared understanding of what the relationship means, but also within this there still needs to be a clear sense of differentiation and respect for each individual. Interdependence allows both parties to thrive; dependence usually means that one thrives at the expense of the other.

FEELING THE PAIN

Of course, despite their fundamental purpose in our lives, our relationships do not always work out. Whilst the original design principles might be clear, young infants do not always get the parents they need and loving relationships can break up and leave us devastated.

Emotional pain inevitably comes from the breakdown of relationships or the loss of those we love. It is a pain which in some cases is even more damaging than physical pain. When we experience emotional pain, the same area of the brain is triggered as if it were physical pain. It is not one location of the brain but is actually referred to as the pain matrix. It is a network of configurations triggered by different types of stimuli causing the sensation of pain.

When we run to achieve some level of personal fitness, endorphins are released into our central nervous system to act as pain relief to enable the exercise to continue. In this way, we often feel the benefit of fitness activity as the endorphins continue to work their way through our bodily system. Unfortunately, the body has no equivalent antidote to emotional pain. Because the evolutionary purpose of emotional pain has been to help us survive, emotions endure because the perceived threat may have endured also. It would be pointless being on alert for a few seconds and then dropping our guard before the threat has disappeared.

So, emotional pain often has to be worked through against a backdrop of long timescales and rational confusion. The body has processes for coping with sadness triggered by loss, or recovering from shock or fear, but in some cases this can take years. We will look at this further later, when we examine traumas and pathologies.

CHAPTER 3.2:

Behavioural Styles

The way we behave and communicate has a major impact on our experience of life. The way we put ourselves out there and the response we get are all part of our social and learning arena and are worthy of consideration in their own right. But it is a subject matter which can also give us an interesting insight into the way we are engaging our brain. For this purpose we revert back to the triune brain and explore how the traits of each of the three layers of the brain can show up in the way we express ourselves. This can be a very user-friendly and accessible place to begin our understanding of how neuroscience principles are demonstrably played out in our lives.

We will explore the rational style of the 'thinker', the energetic style of the 'feeler' and the instinctive style of the 'knower'. Of course, each of these represents the external expression of the features we normally associate with, respectively, the cortex, limbic and basal systems of the brain. I have no interest in pigeon-holing anyone into any of these styles here. The fact is that our behavioural styles are a dynamic blend of all of these styles and we can switch between them in seconds. Nevertheless, the categorisation of styles is helpful in sharpening our awareness, as well as giving us some easy language on which to build interpersonal insights and conversations.

Typically, 'thinking' behaviour will appear as structured and controlled. Thinkers like to think about what they say before they say it and tend to be deliberate in their conversational style. They are comfortable with logic and detail and they like clarity and precision. They seek out the rules and are natural planners, enjoying breaking challenges down to a logical sequence of activities. They tend to be seen as reliable and diligent, albeit maybe ponderous. They are more inclined to be clinical and objective. Typical examples of thinking-dominated professions would be accountants, lawyers, researchers and clinicians.

'Feeling' behaviour will typically be bubbly, outgoing, engaging and prone to mood swings. Feelers can be creative and challenging. They like to respond in the moment, not big on plans or sticking to them, they prefer going with the flow. They are usually active company and enjoy social engagement. Their appearance will often be colourful and expressive. Alternatively, they may express their emotions more passively, such as through empathy and warmth. Whether expressed or subdued, emotional engagement sits at the heart of their behaviour.

The behaviour of knowers is all about taking a position, getting to the point. There is no fuss or undue emotionality in the world of knowing – just do it! Certainty is their trade mark. They know what they want and they just go out and get it. Their action is purposeful and creates an impact. Others can experience this as intolerant or detached. Knowers are decisive and focused and do not welcome any form of distraction, whether it be unnecessary detail or unhelpful emotion. Their conviction can attract people, their arrogance can repel. They want the game played their way or they will not truly engage.

"Preconceived notions are the locks on the door to wisdom."

– Merry Brown

Now think back to the evolutionary story that was explained in Chapter 1. Remember the instinctive reptile, the crocodile (the knower), untrainable but decisive; the energetic mammal, the monkey (the feeler), full of life and curiosity; and the reflective human (the thinker), considering the options and planning his way to success. The parallels between brain region and communication style should be getting clearer.

I hope you will be able to recognise these styles, either distinctly attached to certain people with whom you interact or as fleeting styles we jump into and out of. Each of us will exhibit behavioural tendencies, and when mapped over a longer period of time we may well see that we tend to favour one or two of the styles over the others. We use all three styles throughout our lives. No one style is better than the others. This is not about judgement, it is about observation. Our lives so far have taught us to behave in a particular way; if this choice is serving us perfectly there is no need to consider change, but if we feel we sometimes miss opportunities to connect more effectively with people, a wider appreciation of the styles may come in useful.

Each style would be seen as having both strengths and weaknesses, opportunities both to connect with and disconnect from people. The thinker will tend to be precise, accurate and reliable; others may experience her as unemotional or indecisive. The feeler can be creative and a natural relationship builder. She can energise those around her but she can also drain them. She is easily distracted and does not like rules. The knower is decisive and operates at speed, her conviction creating a sense of certainty in those around her. Yet she stops listening quickly and can be unforgiving of relationships that don't work.

So, a thinker, a feeler and a knower go into a restaurant. The thinker looks at the menu, processes the detail, probably uses some deductive reasoning to narrow down his choice and then, eventually, decides what he will order. The feeler will mainly ignore the menu. She will look around the restaurant, look at what somebody else is eating and see if she fancies it. She will have a word with the waiter and asks what he recommends. Ultimately she will go with mood, which is what she feels. The knower, on the other hand, will take a cursory glance at the menu and zone in quickly for the choices he would expect to make. He orders decisively and without fuss. He then waits impatiently for the others to make their minds up.

How do you spot a thinker shopping? She will usually have a list! Thinkers like plans and structures. They like to put their thoughts down in an orderly process. They like clarity and will execute their actions according to a thought-through process. The feeler goes with the moment. He will be attracted by any energy source that tantalises the senses, such as colour, movement, images and smell. This shopper could well be a victim to the fashion purchase and the spontaneous sale. In the supermarket he will be drawn to the colour and vibrancy of the vegetable and fruit section. What about the knowing shopper? Easy: no fuss! Just get the job done. Know what you want to get, get it, pay for it and get out!

What about our homes? What does a thinker's house look like? And a feeler's? And a knower's? The thinker's will be tidy, organised, everything in its place. CDs will be stacked in order and the cupboards neatly arranged. The feeler's will be 'lived in', which could be anything from untidy to homely. There will be cushions and signs of spontaneity throughout. The knower's home will be minimalist. The knower likes space. Everything should have a purpose and should work. The place should not be cluttered by meaningless or untidy distractions.

The signs of our preferences are everywhere. It could be in the way we eat our meals, the way we play sport, the way we encounter others. Why does this matter? In everyday life it matters because understanding the preferences of those we are trying to communicate with can be critical to making the connection with them. The styles are like different languages. If we speak in 'think' we use detail and tend to be precise and structured in our language. For the thinker it has to make logical sense. The energy of think is neutral, which means it is not animated or excitable, more work-like and matter of fact. Nothing wrong with this, but what if we are trying to communicate with a feeler? Feelers like energy and the neutral tone of the thinker will feel flat, even boring. Feelers are less directly interested in logic or detail. They want to be engaged, energised. Give them colour, pictures and stories. So what chance easy connection between thinker and feeler?

And what about the knower? He just wants you to get to the point. Give him the conclusion and he will instinctively take a position. It's either a yes or a no. There is no sitting on the fence. If he likes the first impression, he may then look for some evidence to back it up (if his secondary style is think) or he may turn to a trusted friend or colleague (if his secondary style is feel) to check it out with them.

So, if the thinker throws detail at the knower or the feeler they will disconnect. If the feeler goes off into storyland with the knower, he will walk away. And the knower's style will typically frustrate the thinker because he does not often explain the rationale behind his thinking or give the facts to back it up. This will equally frustrate the feeler because the message can typically be delivered without compassion or engagement. Here is the answer: take it or leave it!

At this point, I would encourage you to reflect on your own style and how it may impact the relationships in your life. Think about those you easily connect with and those you don't. All too often our ability, or inability, to connect with others will quickly determine whether we become friends or successful colleagues. This initial communication hurdle can be decisive, yet there is so much more to offer each other if we can be more flexible in our communication and our understanding.

The observation and awareness of these styles is also useful at a more scientific level. Each of these styles is giving us a glimpse into which region of the brain is exerting the primary influence when we are trying to communicate. Such an insight is helpful in really understanding where the other person is coming from. If we want to build a communication bridge to another person we have to know where it will land on the other side. Equally, these insights can contribute to our own self-awareness and our understanding of the impact that we have on others, whether positive or negative. The last chapter demonstrated the crucial impact of relationships through our lives; our communication styles are the medium through which these relationships are nourished or damaged.

CHAPTER 3.3:

The Dysfunctional Brain

"Self-conquest is the greatest of victories."

– Plato

ANXIETY RESPONSES

Until now this book has focused on the way the brain is supposed to work, but what happens when things don't go to plan? In this chapter we will look at some of the causes and features of dysfunctional brains, ranging from anxiety disorders to clinical pathologies.

Anxiety is an everyday experience for many people and an occasional experience for most of us: that feeling of twisting and turning in our gut and tightness in our chest. It's not nice and we certainly do not choose it. We know by now that emotions are not a matter of rational choice and can invade our bodies without any conscious warning. Yet humans suffer levels of anxiety which are higher than other species.

This is the downside of our vast thinking capability. Whilst it gives us many advantages, it means we are also able to become fixated by the things that may go wrong in our life. We ponder the future and our ability to visualise many scenarios means we are prone to concocting all sorts of threats – some real and others unlikely. The fact that we can create these negative internal images opens us up to creating our own needless fear responses. Our brains struggle to differentiate between imaginary and real threats and our lives can therefore be led in a state of constant alert.

The same rules apply whether we are concerned about physical threat or social threat. The fear of losing public face is a very powerful trigger and will cause the same reaction in our body, even though there is no physical danger involved. The brain's pain matrix will be activated and the consequences will resonate through our emotional circuitry.

We are capable of thinking about fears but we are incapable of blocking them out. This in part is due to the connectivity of the amygdala. Its connections into the cortex means it can take over our thought processes when the threat level is perceived as high enough. The reverse connections from the cortex to the amygdala do not have the same affect. From an evolutionary perspective this makes sense. It would be dangerous to have a brain that could get so embroiled in thought processing that it fails to respond to threat. Emotions can invade our thoughts but thoughts cannot invade our emotions.

We need to refine our understanding of this a little more. After all, we know that we do not live by our emotions alone. We are constantly moderating our response for the sake of social integration. It would not be a great idea for us to tell our boss exactly what we feel about him, or the police officer or anyone else who may have some authoritative influence on our lives (although it might momentarily be great fun!). So, where does this moderating influence come from?

This is part of the role of the pre-frontal cortex, helping us to keep things in perspective. It does so by integrating emotional and thought data in working memory, thereby giving us a chance to be more measured in our response. When the emotional intensity of an environmental trigger is moderate, the pre-frontal cortex remains in charge and will guide us to a suitable response. When the emotional stakes are raised, especially in relation to a perceived threat, it can sometimes feel like having a tiger by the tail: the emotional force is just too strong to be restrained.

The term 'amygdala hijack' is slowly working its way into popular language. This is a description of the situation where the amygdala is highly aroused (usually by fear but it could also happen in relation to extreme excitement) and high levels of adrenaline are coursing their way through our bodies. The amygdala will direct the brain to focus the flow of oxygenated blood in the brain to the areas required for survival, such as physical response. Finer thoughts are considered luxuries in these situations and considerations of objectivity, sensitivity and wider perspective go out of the window. I am sure that many of us will relate easily to memories when we have 'lost our cool' and reacted in a way that we later considered to be poorly judged.

Yet this behaviour is not dysfunctional; it is exactly as evolution has designed. The problem becomes more problematic when the relative balance between our emotional and cognitive systems becomes distorted so that the see-saw of emotional speed becomes out of kilter with our moderating thought. Anxiety disorders will ensue when the power of our emotions breaks free from the rational influence of the pre-frontal cortex and living on high alert becomes a way of life.

So, whilst we think of fear as an emotion triggered by an external stimulus, anxiety is typically triggered from within. The internal imagery we create in the brain triggers anxious responses and these are just as powerful as those we receive from the outside world. In fact, the brain processes as much as six times more internal visual data as it does external data. We live our lives as an internal movie, connected visually to the external world, but embellished, interpreted and integrated with our own visual stories and memories.

TRAUMA

In many cases, people suffering with anxiety disorders are unable to understand and explain where the fear is coming from. Phenomena such as panic attacks often arise suddenly and without obvious reason. The feeling of imminent doom and the rapid onset of physical symptoms such as sweating, racing heart and shortness of breath can be truly awful for those concerned.

In these cases, the source of the anxiety is not a worrying projection into the future but is more likely to be a real event in the past The type of events that trigger anxiety attacks are emotional experiences that are firmly rooted in the past and are registered so deeply with us that they are firmly tucked away in long-term memory. Often these memories are created in childhood. Remember that for the first three years or so of our lives it is the emotional system of the brain that is accelerating its development the quickest and dominating our everyday life. The cortex is in rapid catch-up but will not have the capability to reflect on and rationalise our experiences. The event therefore goes straight into emotional storage but we have no conscious access to it. Even after the three-year period it will still take some years before our powers of conscious recall become established.

So our early experiences can live with us in memory but they stay below the conscious surface and we feel we have no control of them. Then our day to day experiences may involve encounters where we come across an event which is similar enough to that which is recorded in our unconscious memory. The amygdala spots the match and kicks off the fear response, including an adrenaline and cortisol rush, and we spin into a state of panic. It is particularly difficult because the pre-frontal cortex does not have access to the rational memory data it needs to kick in with its moderating influence; it can't make sense of the reaction and so the anxiety continues and intensifies.

For most panic attack sufferers, the best way to cope with this is to use a routine they have probably already established to calm themselves down, whether it might be breathing into a paper bag to stop hyperventilating, or simply sitting down to avoid further fear stimulation until the physical symptoms gradually subside. It will help if they can go into a routine which triggers a secondary rational assurance that reminds them that they have been through this before and they will get through it this time too.

Ongoing counselling therapy will normally offer sufferers a level of relief, although it may not remove the phenomenon altogether. The aim of conscious therapy in brain terms is to bring memory of the event closer to the sphere of influence of the hippocampus. If we can locate the event by conscious memory recall we can start to mitigate its emotional power by processing the data in a moderating and rational space. Slowly but surely the memory may start to lose its raw power and become less damaging to our lives.

When conscious interaction between counsellor and patient is not working, the therapist may revert to hypnotherapy as an attempt to interact directly with the unconscious mind. This requires skill and trust. The principles are exactly the same as above: it is about bringing memory of the event into the sphere of conscious access via the hippocampus. If this is achieved, the patient will feel that they are regaining some control over their reactions rather than simply being a victim of them.

The same principles apply when we examine post-traumatic stress disorder (PTSD), where the source of the memory may typically manifest in adulthood. Here again, the effect of the traumatic experience is to disable the effective functioning of the hippocampus but it has not because of an underdeveloped cortex.

To understand this, we need to look again at how memories are formed. Here we are not concerned with conscious cognitive memory where we choose to remember something because it is likely to be of practical value in the future. In these circumstances, the brain interaction is primarily between the cortex and the hippocampus. When we experience a significant emotional event, especially if it is sudden and we momentarily feel our life is in danger, cortisol, our primary defensive hormone, floods the body and brain to ward off attack. The problem is that cortisol restricts the activity of the hippocampus and thereby reduces our conscious memory of the event.

As explained earlier, the hippocampus is the filing cabinet of the brain and our main source of conscious memory retrieval. The power of a significant event will undoubtedly be stored in the brain as a neural configuration, but our ability to access it through conscious means is severely restricted. The memory has been stored but not in the filing cabinet. It is somewhere in the memory warehouse but we can't find it.

In this way, the memory is stored in our emotional system and it lurks in our unconscious as a ticking time bomb ready to be triggered whenever any associated event crosses our path. I recall my father still having nightmares 40 years after the Second World War had ended. For some, these nightmares are experienced in waking hours.

The therapeutic principles described above are the same. The memory needs to be brought back into consciousness to allow progress to be made, but here, more than ever, it is an extremely sensitive and tricky path to recovery.

Even though the examples described above are clearly unpleasant for the sufferers, it is still debatable whether the brain is acting in a dysfunctional manner. Given the evolutionary context of survival it is only following its design principles and ensuring that the survival of the species remains at the top of the priorities list. However, there are clear clinical conditions where we can more confidently say that the brain is not operating in a way that was originally intended, so let's have a closer look at these.

CLINICAL DISORDERS

Most illnesses described as 'mental disorders' could actually be termed 'emotional disorders' since they arise when the emotional system overrides the mental (or cognitive) processes of the brain. Anxiety itself is an unresolved fear, an expression of the tensions which arise within the brain itself. Phobias are fears taken to extreme, the source typically being a traumatic memory created in early childhood. There is also evidence that some phobias are learnt from the behaviour of the child's parents. Seeing Mum or Dad reacting fearfully can be as frightening for the child as the parent's object of fear.

Obsessive Compulsive Disorder (OCD) arises when the sufferer resorts to their own rules to get them through their fears. They construct a set of mental and behavioural routines which give them comfort by blocking out the source of fear. This could be excessive washing of hands to block out the fear of infection or dependence on a carefully designed set of behaviours to ward off the fear of social interaction. The greater the fear, the more intense the dependency on the rules.

Autism is a clinically diagnosed condition which can portray some of these behavioural symptoms, but the cause of the problem is much more likely to be genetic. Diagnoses of autism have significantly increased over recent years partly due to better diagnostic capabilities. It also appears to be linked to the growing social trend towards having babies later in life. Research shows a clear correlation between autism, older fathers and difficult pregnancies. Currently, as many as 1% of children are diagnosed as falling within the autism spectrum. The ratio of males to females is 4 to 1. Yet, whilst the research base is growing, there is still so much to be learnt.

It appears that the problem for those diagnosed within the autism spectrum is that there is a breakdown in the neural circuitry that recognises and deals with the more subtle signals of social interaction. Earlier in the book we talked about the vital energetic interaction that goes on between people in any social interaction. There are constant signals that are sensed without involvement from the rational brain. We can sense someone's mood before any language is exchanged. Additionally, our facial recognition system will pick up on all the social cues on offer to make social sense of an occasion.

In cases of autism, the ability to pick up on these cues is missing. The brain's circuitry should initially recognise the signals and enable us to make sense of them. Our limbic system can mirror what it recognises in others and then works in connection with the heart to be able to reproduce what others are feeling. This is the basis of empathy: we literally feel what the other is feeling by creating a similar, if more moderated, sensation in ourselves. In cases of autism there are breakdowns somewhere along the chain between recognition, emotional processing and response.

We speak of the autism spectrum because it is an umbrella diagnosis that recognises the symptoms of behavioural and social dysfunction. Yet the neural causes may vary anywhere along this chain. As yet, intervention at the neurological level is very limited since we are on such a steep learning curve. Dealing with the behavioural symptoms and distress falls instead to parents and primary care givers and typically this entails understanding the condition rather than changing it since solutions are not available through behaviour modification or traditional therapy. It is more a case of recognising what the individual has to do to feel safe in his environment and respecting these rules and boundaries.

Many theories abounded in the early days of autism diagnoses but the emerging understanding now points to the belief that people suffering with autism experience 'amygdala overload'. The amygdala is a central hub in our ability to process emotional data; it allocates emotional value to any given environmental trigger thereby allowing us to prioritise. If the value is low we can partly set it aside as a minor encumbrance; if it is high it demands immediate attention and response.

In autism cases, this prioritisation process has broken down and everything seems important. When we are unable to distinguish between the major and the minor, the emotional system goes into overload and creates intense feelings of fear. It is deeply upsetting to see sufferers going through these episodes. Their brains are bombarded with emotional trauma and they do not have access to the moderating influences of the pre-frontal cortex to regain perspective and calm. All they have is the rules they have created for themselves, their familiar and fragile routines which slowly neutralise the intense negative energy they are experiencing. They live life on a tightrope of emotional balance with the behavioural rules of survival reflected in the delicate safety net that sits perilously far below.

Schizophrenia has been diagnosed for many years but its treatment has varied as the theoretical basis of understanding the condition has evolved. Therapeutic intervention has shown negligible benefits and psychiatric treatment was normally focused on ameliorating the symptoms. Now, with modern technology and science, we can be more confident that the cause of the problem is a chemical imbalance within the brain.

Psychosis is an extreme emotional state, where the gravity of fear is so intense that the sufferer's fundamental sense of self erodes to the point of collapse. It is a disorder in which thought and emotions are so polarised that contact is lost with external reality. The sufferer typically lives in their own imaginary world either episodically or permanently. In the absence of effective connection with the external environment, the psychotic brain turns inwards and creates and responds to its own internal imagery. In this way, psychopaths are unable to relate to their victims, there being no emotional connection and no empathy. They are dehumanised and seen simply as an object, a transaction to be executed.

Unfortunately, similar principles have been used intentionally in cases of psychological torture. Sensory deprivation, such as prolonged solitary confinement, results in the victim losing contact with the real external world. The brain cannot cope with a vacuum and so it turns inwards to an imaginary world, a hallucinatory existence. Such a breakdown in our own sense of self and how we interact with our environment will make us desperately vulnerable to further interrogation.

In all of these cases, our understanding of the causes of clinical disorders has been substantially enhanced by recent findings in neuroscience. Pathological study has been a critical contributor to our understanding of the brain. Still a relatively young science, it is building a scientific knowledge base which is already dramatically expanding our ability to create neurological interventions for the treatment of disorders. This is indeed a cause for great optimism.

But before we leave this section I would like to take a quick look at dementia.

Dementia cannot be described as a genetic disorder in the sense that it is not about the brain operating incorrectly as such but more about the very natural process of aging. For those who suffer with dementia this is no source of comfort but again science is throwing new light on our understanding of the condition.

It appears that one of the prime causes of dementia is the build-up of plaque deposits impacting the connective capacity of the synapses in the brain. This is like the furring up on any electrical connection. When the connection is corroded the quality deteriorates and directly impacts our thinking ability and access to language and memory. As the condition progresses, symptoms will include mood swings and disorientation. Eventually it can impact areas such as physical functioning and movement.

Another significant cause is trauma, such as the impact of a stroke or head injury. In this case, blood supply to the brain is restricted and the consequent oxygen deficit means that our brain cells cease to function. This is vascular dementia and can also be caused by the natural effects of aging.

Dementia is an umbrella terms used to denote the typical symptoms described above. Alzheimer's is one form of dementia, a condition which can be equally frightening for sufferers and loved ones alike. Central to this condition is loss of memory and the ruthless nature of its impact on those involved brings up the whole issue of 'personality'. Primary care givers of those suffering with Alzheimer's or dementia often comment that the sufferer is no longer the person they once knew; they have been 'lost'. This is an incredibly difficult experience and can cause great frustration in continuing to relate to the person they are now caring for. They feel the person they love is still 'in there somewhere' but they can't get access to them.

My mother was strong enough to live to the age of 91, and whilst dementia did eventually catch up with her, it was only in her last few years and the symptoms remained mild. Things changed in the last month before her death. It was difficult to see her memories disappearing in front of my eyes. It started with more recent memories and then chipped away at her whole life history. I recall sitting with her at the hospital and her thinking that I was her Dad. She was asking not to go to school that day because she didn't feel well.

When anyone sees someone they love gradually disappear from view and become a shell-like impersonation of what they once were it is likely to have a profound effect. The big impact for me was the painful realisation of just how important our memory is to who we are and everything we do. I knew this beforehand but I had never felt it with such depth.

Today, I set aside much conversation about personality. For me it is about our memories and the way we have made sense of them in our lives to date. This is our life story and is a direct representation of the way the connectivity of our brain has been nurtured, both consciously and unconsciously, throughout our lives. When we contemplate the future we project this historically based view of self into imagined future circumstances and evaluate how the 'I' we know now would be likely to respond. Without memory there is nothing to project, no platform for making sense of what lies ahead. Hence, the devastating effects on those whose memories are denied them by the impact of dementia.

Dysfunctionality can appear in many forms. Synaesthesia is a condition where our sensory intelligence systems appear to become cross-wired. There are many reported examples of this.

In one case, a person 'sees' sounds; when she hears particular types of sounds (usually musical), distinct images are evoked in her brain with specific colours and patterns. I recently met someone who 'smelt' colours; for her the colour orange was particularly powerful in evoking a distinct aroma. In these cases the reaction was not created through cognitive interpretation or imagination but through direct sensory links.

On the other hand, the brain is able to self-heal to a degree by the process we call neural plasticity. This refers to the brain's ability to regenerate new cells to recover function. This could be on a small, localised level or, more exceptionally, on a more dramatic scale. We know that, in certain circumstances, it will use one part of the brain to compensate for the loss of function in another part. There are recorded cases of people having major parts of one side of their brain surgically removed to prevent further disease. In some cases, the remaining side of the brain adapted its own development to compensate for the loss and to recover some of the sensory intelligence that would otherwise have been lost. This immense flexibility can sometimes go awry and these curious examples of sensory cross-wiring will occur.

Another curiosity is that of sleepwalking (somnambulism). Most of us are aware of this and have encountered someone who has suffered from the condition. It is a rather surreal experience encountering someone in the sleepwalking state: they display a marginal sense of consciousness but with none of the facial responses we normally associate with waking behaviour. They are there, but not there. My son has been a sleepwalker since his teenage years and still has to endure this now he is in his thirties; typically it happens at times when he is most animated (usually business pressure!) and when he is running on high alert.

It appears that sleepwalking occurs when the normal neural mechanisms for waking us up from dreams are not effectively activated. As we discussed earlier, the limbic region of the brain never sleeps; it is the region of the brain where we activate dreams. The thinking brain, however, will go into voluntary standby mode and preserve its energy. In normal sleep patterns we will progress through the dreaming stages of our sleep without any conscious awareness of the dreams themselves unless we are woken up. If we have unduly stressful dreams or nightmares, our cognitive system will be triggered back into life and will wake us up. I am sure we can relate to those moments when we first wake from a dream and reality takes a few seconds to take over from the dream experience.

In cases of sleepwalking, the waking mechanism is not effective and instead of being pulled out of the dream, the hallucinatory experience continues. The sleepwalker is literally living out his dream. Fortunately, in most circumstances, the sleepwalker comes to no harm and no damage is done other than a sense of disorientation when his behaviour is described to him the next morning. However, regrettably, there have been extreme cases where people have lost their lives through walking unconsciously into danger and even the case of Ken Parks in America in 1987 who drove 20 miles to kill members of his family while in a sleepwalking state. He was found innocent of murder. Thank goodness such cases are mercifully rare.

INTERVENTION AND THERAPIES

In this chapter we have looked at instances when the brain becomes dysfunctional. The causes of this dysfunction range from genetic to cultural. There is ample evidence to show cases where parents have passed on a genetic condition to their children, such as a propensity towards addictive behaviour. This does not necessarily mean that the child will inevitably suffer from the same condition. It will depend on the child's experience of life. If the conditions she experiences in life are arduous this may well trigger addictive behaviour as the relevant genes are activated by this circumstance.

On the other hand, the child may pass through life without encountering the conditions which activate the gene. In this case, the latent condition will remain dormant.

We also know that some phobias are learnt by children from their parents, that is to say the fear was not a genetic precondition but became embedded in memory as a consequence of seeing and feeling how Mum or Dad had reacted when they themselves encountered a particular fear stimulus. If Mum is constantly terrified of spiders and demonstrates an extreme reaction in the company of a young child there is a distinct possibility that the child herself will remember the same fear and respond in a similar way.

So what of therapeutic interventions? Over recent years this has mainly involved treatments such as cognitive based therapy (CBT), psychotherapy or some other psychologically based discipline. Yet the rate of sustainable success has been mixed. Of course, practitioners have been working with great intent and with the knowledge available to them at the time, but emerging neuroscience is helping us better understand exactly what they have been up against.

The biggest challenge has probably been the emphasis of these therapies on conscious interventions. This means that they have relied to a great extent on a process of rational dialogue and exchange where they are supporting their client to become more consciously aware of the conditions that trigger their anxieties and their own internal and behavioural responses to these conditions. This is absolutely the right thing to do and it is only by bringing our experiences into consciousness that we are able to deal with them at the rational level. However, as has been described earlier, the problematic memory typically resides at the unconscious level and normal access via the hippocampus is denied.

Such therapeutic intervention invariably relies on conscious memory recall: the therapist helps the client to reconnect with the memory that appears to be causing the problem. However, this type of recall can be very unreliable. Emotional memory captures the feeling rather than the detail, yet when we look back we are notoriously inclined to fill in the gaps according to how we feel now. We are naturally inclined to rationalise our experiences from the way we are making sense of life now but we are not the people we were when the memory was created. It's a form of rewriting history.

Likewise, the process of memory recovery itself can be treacherous. We know reconstruction of traumatic memories can be crucial in facing our past fears, yet we can also be opening up a can of worms. Any attempt to retrospectively make sense may not have access to the real trigger. We are seeking access through the hippocampus and the cognitive system but the memory has been created by the intervention of the amygdala and the emotional system. Emotional responses can be triggered at a subliminal level without conscious awareness of the stimulus and so any attempt to understand retrospectively is fraught with the danger of misdiagnosis.

There is general recognition in therapeutic spheres of the power of narrative. We can learn so much from the way that someone tells us their story. Sharing language gives us a structure for communication and mutual understanding, and listening to the way that someone has pieced together their experiences can be very insightful. Yet, even here, there are dangers of misrepresentation. There are occasions when the language of post-rationalisation becomes the barrier to authenticity.

As therapists or coaches we have a fine line to tread when we are invited by our clients to buy into their view of life. Of course, it is vital that we do our best to understand it and this is best done by trying to share their mindset. We are trying to climb into their brains and see the world from their perspective. This is a basis for connection and empathy but it should not mean that we buy into it. Part of our role is to retain such a level of interdependence that we can reflect back to them possible different takes on the way they have made sense of their lives so far. If we simply 'go native' with their explanation we have become only an extension of their own rationalisation, so what is the point of the therapy or coaching conversation?

Partly this challenge is about moving beyond the narrative. When asked the classic question 'so how did you feel about…?' the response is typically what we *think* about. Our client has made sense of his emotions by wrapping them up in a rational narrative. We can be of more use if we encourage them to stop rationalising and instead get them to name the emotions they actually experienced. We can support them better if we get beyond the rational system and start dealing directly with the emotional system, which is less about carefully constructed logic and more about spontaneous expression and energetic connection. Sharing the feeling on an emotional level can be more powerful than sharing the logic used to make sense of it. Making sense of this sharing will follow but it should not dictate the parameters.

Emotional access is a prerequisite to personal change. Staying in the land of the rational is comfortable but only reaffirms the way we see things now. At the same time, having gained emotional access we need to tread wisely and sensitively; then, when the time is right, we need to steer the conversation back into the rational domain of working memory so that we can regain perspective and learn. In brain terms, having got closer to the emotional source of the problem we now need to give the pre-frontal cortex a chance to re-engage through working memory. Ultimately, therapeutic interventions are about supporting the cortex to exert influence over the emotional system as a whole and the amygdala in particular. But beware, it can be like grabbing a tiger by the tail!

The ongoing battle of influence between the emotional and rational systems is by no means limited to clinically diagnosed disorders. We have to deal with this on a daily basis. Emotional moderation is a prerequisite for social cohesion. If we all said what we felt without considering the impact, our lives would be very fractious. It is the natural role of the pre-frontal cortex to be sensitive to this and to help us find socially appropriate expression for our feelings. But what happens when emotional moderation becomes emotional suppression?

The position becomes unhealthy when moderation becomes suppression and we find we have to consistently bottle up our feelings. We are building an emotional dam in the brain and closer examination will reveal flaws in the dam that will break if the emotional torrent becomes too fierce. Emotional outbursts will inevitably follow, sometimes at the least expected time, not necessarily because of the specific emotional trigger but simply because the dam could cumulatively take no more. Taken to extreme, such suppression can become very destructive and the dam breaks.

The tensions that we play out in life are themselves a direct reflection of the tensions we experience in the brain. I am sure we can relate to many instances when we have wanted to express ourselves freely but we have chosen at a rational level to approach matters more diplomatically. Likewise, we are likely to be faced with situations of conflict between our sexual instincts and our resultant behaviour. If we are attracted to someone sexually, our instincts will be triggered instantaneously. We may find it easy to ignore this or it may be a stronger feeling that persists. If we are committed to an existing relationship, attraction to a new person will present us with a moral dilemma. What we decide to do next is entirely our call but the sexual attraction remains a reality no matter how much behavioural camouflage we construct to misrepresent the situation.

We can see this tension in the brain being played out at a more extreme level when we are examining drug or alcohol addiction. Taking of drugs or alcohol is a process of immediate gratification: we do it because we want a particular effect now, whether it is one of relaxation, excitement or release. Over time some people develop a habit of doing this and gradually a level of dependence is built up. Eventually this dependence becomes physiological and the brain demands more of the same. This gratification is an emotional phenomenon: we do it because of the way it makes us feel now.

This represents the battle which is taking place between our rational and emotional systems. The limbic brain operates in the here and now and demands its 'fix'. The cortex is invaded and unable to stem the power of the emotional system. When the initial surge of the drug or alcohol input subsides, the cortex attempts the process of rational recovery. The rehabilitation process then becomes a contest to extend the influence of the cortex and reduce the demands of the emotional system. Therapeutic analysis is therefore focused on bringing awareness of the triggers of the condition back into the conscious domain of the pre-frontal cortex. This is the only chance of self-imposed moderation.

From a brain perspective, the problem goes deeper than this. If we 'choose' to suppress our feelings on a constant basis then this inevitably means suppressing all feelings. The brain cannot differentiate emotions at this level so if we block them we have to block the lot. This means we have to become de-sensitised to what is going on around us. In aggressive conditions this can mean we have become 'brutalised' to our environment. Those having to cope with the demands of warfare have learnt that switching off their feelings is the only way to cope.

Ongoing anxiety will lead to wider neural damage. General stress reduces our anxiety threshold leaving us more vulnerable to future damage. It also reduces the moderating influence of the pre-frontal cortex, which in turn makes us more prone to emotional outbursts and panic attacks. Prolonged anxiety causes degeneration of cells in the hippocampus leading to memory loss. Cognitive memory is worst affected whilst, on the other hand, emotional fears remain indelible, designed to keep us alive but impossible to eradicate.

Over recent years, we have started to see an expansion of direct neurological interventions. Initially this was primarily for clinical purposes aimed at minimising the impact of brain disease or trauma. More recently, as the confidence of the profession grows, neuroscience is introducing wider clinical interventions with encouraging effects.

One example of this is Trans Magnetic Stimulation (TMS) where electrodes are placed across the skull to use electrical charges to stimulate particular patterns of brain activity. This has produced some very positive results in the treatment of autism. We are aware that one cause of autism is a breakdown in the neural connectivity that links our emotional and rational systems. It appears that this treatment reactivates this connectivity and re-fires the relevant networks. It is early days but the implications are very significant.

CHAPTER 3.4:

Stress, Resilience and Belief

"Until you make peace with who you are, you will never be content with what you have."

– Doris Mortman

In the previous chapter we looked at anxiety responses from the viewpoint of what was going on in the brain. In this chapter we will broaden this to a wider exploration of stress. It is helpful to think of anxiety as a response which is triggered by a specific stimulus, whereas stress is an accumulated condition, a more generalised state of (largely negative) alert and discontentment. This means that we need to extend the scope of the discussion since, as most of us know to our cost, stress is not a cerebral experience. It is not a sensation which is confined to the brain, it is deeply rooted in our bodies. We therefore need to return to our understanding of the body's wider intelligence system.

THE THREAT RESPONSE MECHANISM

I explained earlier the role of the amygdala in triggering our response to threat. When the amygdala perceives a threat it activates a chain reaction which gears the body to react in the desired way. In behavioural terms this reaction will include freezing (our instantaneous response to sudden threat), fleeing or fighting and facial expression.

Internally the threat response mechanism is a visceral experience, impacting organs, glands and the hormonal system. At the instant of perceived threat, hormone secretion will be activated via the hypothalamus and pituitary gland. Amongst other things, this will potentiate rapid eye movement and piloerection (hairs rising) as our senses are alerted and we turn our attention immediately to identify the source of the threat. At this point there is minimal input from the cortex to the amygdala, but neural connections from the amygdala to the cortex will allow it to demand attention and dictate perception. In times of threat the amygdala is king and there is no room for rational distraction.

Endorphins will quell physical pain during the initial response as pain itself could be a distraction from our route to survival. (If you have ever been involved in a fight, you will know that much of the initial pain goes unnoticed but it will kick in quickly afterwards!)

The threat stimulus triggers the Automatic Nervous System (ANS), which is the part of our wider nervous system and regulates most of the autonomic (automatic) systems within our body. These systems would include respiration, heart rate, blood circulation, hunger and thirst, temperature control and the hormonal system. ANS regulation is effected either through the sympathetic pathway when there is a need to speed up the systems, or through the parasympathetic pathway when the need is to slow down. The sympathetic system relates to our 'fight or flight' response, whereas the parasympathetic system relates to 'rest and digest'.

As the ANS is activated, adrenaline is secreted from the adrenal glands and the heart becomes highly aroused as it prepares the body for immediate response. Adrenaline here acts as the priming agent, or petrol, of the body. Blood circulation is increased, and signals are sent through the motor-neural nervous system (which controls our muscles and movement) to generate the required physical response. All of this happens in a split second.

We have all experienced this, the momentary response when we find our heart bursting and our senses primed. We will stay in this state until we believe the threat has subsided. At this point, adrenaline production will reduce and another hormone, acetylcholine, will takes its place to bring about a calming response. This is the body's way of 'warming down' and resuming normal operation. So, we can think of adrenaline as the accelerator of our body and acetylcholine as the brake. If used well together, they will take us through life navigating the scenarios we encounter with natural response and optimised energy. Problems arise when we try using the brake and accelerator at the same time: we put our systems under significant pressure as we burn out the brakes and the tyres and damage the engine.

The chain reaction is similar when we perceive an opportunity, but with important differences. Whereas the perception of threat triggers the survival response, the perception of opportunity generates excitement and is experienced as a positive sensation. Initially, the ANS response is the same in triggering adrenaline to prime the body for action. But it doesn't stay the same. We all know that our emotional experience of threat is very different from that of excitement. So whilst the first part of the priming process is the same, the next stage of the chain reaction is fundamentally different.

Here we have to understand the function of two particular hormones: cortisol and dehydroepiandrosterone (DHEA). Cortisol is often referred to as the body's 'stress hormone'. When the initial scenario which triggered the amygdala response is perceived as threatening, the body primes itself for attack. Cortisol is a natural defence hormone whose function is to fight off threat of trauma and infection. It is an anti-inflammatory and will be directed to those parts of the body perceived to be under attack. It therefore forms a critical part of our immune system response. People in sport will recognise the use of cortisone (a synthetic form of cortisol) injections to ease the pain and swelling of injuries. Its role therefore is entirely protective.

DHEA, on the other hand, is triggered when the expectation is of a positive experience. This could range from the hunter sensing the kill; the opportunity to make love with someone to whom we are highly attracted; or the chance to make a critical point in a public debate. DHEA is a key component in the production of oestrogen and testosterone and fundamental in the body's reproductive system. It is a core part of the life-creation process. When released into the body, the effects are entirely positive, giving energy and a deep sense of achievement and satisfaction. Just as cortisone is available synthetically as a painkilling agent, DHEA has also been used in the treatment of fertility and anti-ageing treatments.

So, to re-cap: the perception of threat or opportunity will trigger a physiological chain reaction throughout the body. If we perceive a threat, cortisol will be released to protect us from attack. If the perception is positive, DHEA will be triggered and we will feel we can conquer the world! Acetylcholine will help us to resume normal operation when the initial trigger has subsided.

STRESS AND RESILIENCE

Whilst we have looked here at the specific threat response reaction within our intelligence system, we cannot think of these as occasional events. Life is about a continuous stream of responses to stimuli, an ongoing flow of internal traffic to be navigated through our bodies. It is these cumulative effects which will determine whether our ongoing experience is one of stress or resilience.

Stress comes about when the demand on our physiological resources outweighs our ability to supply, thus putting us under pressure. This upsets our natural state of balance (homeostasis) and drains the body's energy supply. As we have already seen in the previous references to anxiety triggers, stress can bring with it emotional pain which can be as damaging in the longer term as physical pain but without the natural antidotes provided by endorphins. Stress impacts both physical and intellectual performance and impairs memory. The preponderance of cortisol in our blood system limits the impact of oxytocin, a critical hormone in our sense of well-being.

Ongoing health depends upon us using our energy wisely. Anxiety and stress are examples of the sub-optimisation of energy, a precious commodity we cannot afford to waste. When in a state of alarm we are sending energy to all areas of our body while we seek out the threat. If this continues over the longer term our internal systems will deteriorate and eventually cease to perform. In contrast, when we are calm and positive our energy is focused, optimised and, in the longer term, we are able to build energy reserves for the challenges ahead. So the way we manage our energy is critical, and central to our exploration of human energy management is the role played by our hearts.

Once considered little more than a sophisticated pump for circulating blood around the body, the evidence now emerging is of a sophisticated neurological unit performing a critical role in maintaining the physiological balance of the body. Most of the heart's work is performed unconsciously, that is without conscious input from the cortex. For the most part, the heart operates according to its own independent operating instructions.

In terms of the human energy management system, the heart can be considered the powerhouse of the human body. It generates approximately 50 times the electrical output of the brain, supplying more than 2.5 watts of power. It generates an electromagnetic signal which is at least 1,000 times greater than that of the brain. Its electrical signal is distributed to every cell in our body.

The electrical output of the heart has become a critical measure in the monitoring of our cardiovascular health, typically by the use of the electrocardiogram (ECG). The level of output and variability of our heart rhythms is hugely informative in the diagnosis of health risks and treatments. Each heartbeat provides the trained specialist with a rich source of data. By tracking the level and frequency of the heart's electrical output we are able to gain vital insights into our physical health.

The electrical beat of the heart triggers energetic reactions throughout the body. It uses energy as a communication medium. This introduces us to the concept of energetic entrainment. The radiation of the heart's beat acts as a central point of electromagnetic synchronisation for other neurological units in the body. The body is a total organism and it is the heart which physiologically regulates the performance of the whole, the orchestra conductor who synchronises the constituent parts and produces the sound that matters. By producing a particular level of electrical output at a specific frequency, the heart calls the neurological units of the body into line to create the total effect.

To continue the analogy, the musicians in this orchestra are the cranial brain, the enteric brain and the neurological units responsible for respiration and blood circulation. Without the heart's intervention they are largely independent units following their own path. Yet, when the heart steps up to conduct, the orchestra follows. The conductor sets the pace and rhythm. Each musician has his or her music sheet to follow, instructions specific to the performance of the instrument concerned. Yet, without a conductor, the total effect of all the musicians performing to their own instructions is likely to be less than pleasing, and certainly not as good as it could be. The heart is the grand conductor of orchestral energy.

In our everyday lives this means that our hearts perform at the most optimal level when we are in a state of calm. This becomes a self-reinforcing effect as no energy is wasted on pointless worries. Resilience in this sense is the ability to access and maintain this place of inner calmness where we feel no sense of being threatened, where we instinctively use our energy for worthwhile causes. In this state, we not only optimise our energy but also build up a reserve for future needs. We are travelling, yet filling the petrol tank as we go along. Our resilience threshold will increase as the reserves accumulate and problems which may have worried us at a lower threshold point now seem insignificant.

The implications of these observations are very significant when we come to look at personal performance potential in the next chapter.

INTERPERSONAL IMPACT

When I was studying at university in the 70s I recall coming across research which showed that for many years dentists as a profession had traditionally suffered with an unusually high mortality rate. Whilst being a well-paid profession, their survival beyond retirement age was much less than other professions. At that time psychologists put this down to 'stress transfer'. By dealing with stressed patients on a daily basis it was considered inevitable that the dentists themselves would suffer accumulative stress. The theory was centred mainly on a psychological experience, which means that the mental experience of coping with this would itself, over a period of time, cause the dentist to become stressed. It all seems very logical and I am sure it still makes sense. However, current technology has shown us that something else is also happening.

The issue is also one of the physical proximity of the respective hearts of the dentist and patient. I have explained above that the heart radiates electromagnetic energy to every cell in our bodies. In fact, this electromagnetic effect extends beyond our bodies, typically to an extent of at least five feet. This means that each of us is surrounded by our own electromagnetic field generated by our hearts.

When we move into close proximity of each other these magnetic fields directly connect. This translates into a form of direct communication between the respective hearts, in this case those of the dentist and patient. Laboratory research has shown that the heart rhythms of the patient are directly transmitted to the heart of the dentist while in this close proximity. It's like holding an active mobile phone to the radio – the result is audible interference. Only in the case of the dentist there is no visible or audible sign and only appropriately placed electrical sensors can display the effects. The cumulative effect on the dentist in these circumstances will be a build-up of stress as the heart's normal rhythms are impacted by those of anxious patients.

For me, this represents a great parallel for the impact of neurological data on traditional psychology. It is not that the psychologists of the last century were wrong or incompetent, far from it. It was more directly that they were not able to support their theories with data from live brains. Current research data, including functional MRI scans, has gone a long way to overcoming this limitation. Instead of developing theories based on statistical correlations of observed behaviour patterns we now have the opportunity to examine brain activity directly in relation to specific triggers, behaviours and experiences. We are moving from an observational model to an explanatory model.

So we now understand that our impact on each other in social situations is not just a psychological experience, it also takes place at the physical energetic level. The impact we have on each other is significant. We can energise one another or we can drag each other down. When we are surrounded by people who support us we can use their energy to sustain our own resilience. When we are in a hostile or uncaring environment the opposite is true: we are constantly battling with the energy-sapping effects created by those around us.

SOCIAL CONFLICT AND COHESION

Any conflict that exists in society is an expression of the conflict we feel in our own brains, the external manifestation of our inner feelings. This theme of brain conflict runs deep on a very personal level. In an earlier chapter I described confidence as alignment between our thoughts, feelings and instincts, a state which takes us into 'the zone'. Yet this is a state most of us access only rarely, if ever. Our inner experience of our daily reality is more one of tension between these areas and life itself is the journey of navigation along this tortuous route.

A regular conflict is played out between our thoughts and our emotions. The most obvious example of this is the way we have constructed such elaborate behaviours and language to moderate the social impact of our emotions. I often hear the phrase 'honesty is the best policy' but reflection suggests this to be a dangerous mantra in modern society. I am sure we are all seduced by the idea of being more honest and transparent with each other, but I would not recommend you suddenly live your life solely by this creed and without consideration of the social impact of such behaviour. Let's be serious, if we really expressed what we felt in the moment, we would introduce emotional turmoil into our lives and the lives of others. Far from being emotionally productive, we would be likely to open up a hurtful can of worms that few of us have the resilience to handle. So we try to achieve an acceptable balance where we are able to express ourselves appropriately but without making matters worse.

This tension is not limited to the battle of emotions and rationale; we also see it played out in terms of instincts versus thoughts. Consider sexual attraction. Society demands that we display any physical attraction to another individual only in the most discreet and appropriate circumstances. Marriage and other long-term relationships are predicated on a vow of loyalty, which means such publically displayed attraction to others is not acceptable at a social level. Yet sexual attraction is not a rational choice, it is an instinctive response. If we are sexually attracted to someone we cannot will it away; we can choose to behave in a way that keeps our instincts to ourselves but that will not make them disappear.

So we are left with the need to manage the dilemma as best we can. If the attraction is a result of a fleeting meeting or glance, it should be easy to set aside and to behave in the manner that will protect our existing commitments and relationships. But if the 'opportunities' are repeated, such as at work or at a social venue, the power of the temptation may overcome the more considered choice. It is no surprise then that the majority of illicit affairs occur between existing friends or between work colleagues.

We spend so much of our lives suppressing our instincts and emotions as the necessary price for social cohesion and relationships. Overdone, this becomes unhealthy as we try to live out the conflict on an entirely internalised level. Whilst I challenge the simplicity of the honesty mantra, I do believe our happiness depends on being who we really are. Once again, this is an integral challenge of life's journey and inevitably the pursuit of the Holy Grail is one of striking the right balance.

Whatever the inner tension, the battle for achieving moderation or balance is fought within the conscious realm of the pre-frontal cortex. By momentarily retaining and integrating emotional and instinctive data in working memory we have learnt to be more considered in our behavioural choices. This is a positive trend in that it gives our species the opportunity to make more rational choices about the types of society we want to build for the future. On the other hand, addressing rational choices without addressing emotional and instinctive needs is like building castles in the sand.

RESILIENCE AND BELIEF

The people we interact with on a daily basis are therefore a potential source of resilience for us if we share a sense of mutual support and alignment. We are on the same side. This is a very useful external source of energy particularly accessible by our emotional systems. Yet there is an internal source of resilience accessible only by ourselves – that of belief. Nobody can do this for us; it is our world, our experience and our reality. When we believe in what we are doing we have a sense of inner purpose. When we have this purpose we are internally aligned at the instinctive level. We are where we belong. This is a theme I want to explore further in a later chapter as it deserves more attention.

For now, it is about recognising that when we have belief we are referencing inner images and sensations that give us energy rather than take it away. This is a state of inner honesty, uncluttered by the distractions and falsities of ego. This subject runs deep and impacts us on a daily basis.

We have already looked at the development of the human brain in an earlier chapter and this showed that the pre-frontal cortex does not reach full maturity until about the age of 24 years. However, the experience of our teenage years and the associated hormonal and physical changes invariably increases the pressure on us to search out our own identity. We are undergoing the natural transition away from dependence on our parents and are, in parallel, competing with the social demands of being acknowledged by our peers, who themselves are facing all the same uncertainties. If we do not adopt a position in our lives it may feel like some sort of vortex; the dilemma is that our view of ourselves is still maturing and so positions we take are fraught with the danger of superficiality and misrepresentation. We feel the need to find ourselves but often do not have the wherewithal to access the deeper self-knowledge which will give us the personal meaning we are seeking.

It is in this void that the ego emerges. Here I am not using the word ego in any judgemental sense, as is so often implied nowadays as a state of self-promotion and narrowness of perspective. I am using it more in the Freudian sense of it being the image of ourselves we choose to show to the world. The problem arises when this ego we have adopted turns out not to be a true representation of who we really are. We are then left to balance the tension between the role we have chosen to play and our inner truth.

This is not some fanciful notion. When we are playing a false game, no matter how subtle, we can sense our own internal tensions and are left with a feeling of emptiness. We may choose to play a game of elaborate self-deception and even sometimes manage to convince ourselves that this is OK. But this feeling will not last. Sophisticated cognitive games may get us through some immediate obstacles but if we are not true to ourselves this will come at a cost. Maybe initially this cost is acceptable in the game of social survival but it will accumulate to a point where daily tension becomes the name of the game.

In these circumstances our life becomes a reflection of the contradictions we are experiencing in the brain. Our cognitive system may have adopted an ego position which appears on the surface to be tactically appropriate, but if our feelings are telling us something else we have created an inner conflict which will cause distress and waste energy. Typically these could be feelings of anxiety and defensiveness as we contemplate the threat of exposure or loss of social standing. Shame, as discussed in an earlier chapter, is an especially relevant emotion here. The ego is often intended as our very own fortress for keeping us safe from the threat of social shame. The downside is this particular fortress can also become our prison, our own place of isolation where we withdraw from the siege of danger sitting outside the castle walls, yet only to find ourselves deteriorate from starvation on the inside.

Contrast this with situations of genuine fulfilment, where we are succeeding by being ourselves. We have a sense of purpose which motivates us and gives us direction. Reflect on your body's state at these times; after some initial excitement, it is likely to be calm and peaceful. We know we are playing out who we really are. Our inner intelligence systems will be totally synchronised and energy focused on what we know we can achieve. Our bio-feedback mechanisms embedded in our bodies will be signalling to the brain that everything is OK. We are on track and using our energy for a meaningful purpose; our heart rhythms will be coherent and orchestrating the neurological musicians to create inner harmony.

There is no risk of social exposure when we are being true to ourselves.

INTERVENTIONS

There are many techniques in use for psychological intervention in human behaviour and probably an even wider selection of physiological interventions. People are in a constant search for antidotes to stress and anxiety. I would suggest that there are typically three levels of personal intervention we can choose into our own responses and behaviour patterns.

The most common is behavioural control. This means that we are trying to constrain ourselves to a deliberate, preconsidered behavioural response, sometimes described as 'keeping your grip'. Curiously, like so many of these phrases, it is very apt as it implies keeping a grip or lid on our emotions. At this level, emotions are something to be kept in the private space of our own bodies rather than matters for public display. And, of course, without some compliance to these rules society could not function.

When we are 'controlling' minor or even moderate emotions this can be done easily and without any unnecessary bodily discomfort. Yet, when the anxiety stakes rise, the more difficult the task becomes and the cracks in our social mask begin to appear. When we are internalising powerful emotions, the negative energetic source will be retained inside us, only to be resurrected every time there is a memory association that is triggered. So, behaviour control, whilst socially essential, can also be the source of health decline. The problem with this type of intervention is that it is enacted only at the very end of the behavioural response cycle; that is, the emotional response has already been triggered and the potential for health damage already realised. So we have to examine ways of intervening in our responses earlier.

If we want to get ahead in the emotional response game, the first thing we can do is get to understand and spot the triggers. Each of us will have built through life our programmed responses to those situations or people that attract us, threaten us or sadden us. It can be very productive to be clear about what exactly these triggers are. When it comes to negative triggers, we can sometimes find it difficult to analyse them rationally because of the associative emotion attached to the experience. Yet, there is value to be gained in reflection here, when the intensity of the pain has died down, to try retrospectively to spot patterns in our defensive responses. No doubt, many of these conditioned responses are well founded and appropriate to maintain, but some may be irrational, currently irrelevant and putting us through needless anxiety.

As we spot these unnecessary instances and patterns, we need to rewrite the rules in the brain. The rules we have already laid down are no longer serving us and need to be removed or rewritten. If they are deeply ingrained this may not be easy to achieve but there will be others that are not so deep but are just as inhibiting. They need to be flushed out. The more we explain to ourselves that our conditioned response to these triggers is no longer necessary, the more we will convince our brains that it is OK to drop our guard in relation to this particular issue. By doing this we are facilitating the increased scope of our rational system over our emotional system. We are bringing the problem into consciousness. The old rules were only ever written to protect us, so don't get angry, just get updated!

It is then a matter of getting ahead of the game emotionally by spotting the triggers as soon as they come on to your personal radar. This may seem like a contradiction as, as explained earlier in the book, this is exactly what the amygdala does. The difference here is that you are looking for the trigger and have the rewritten response (the rational case for dismissing the threat) ready to hand. The brain will gradually learn to access the new 'solution' and the risk of the threat response is reduced. You are training the brain to turn a previously held fear response into a rational and currently appropriate reaction.

So, identifying the likely triggers to our emotional responses will give us the first defence against unhelpful reactions, yet there is no way that such a defence can be impregnable. There will always be those threats which will penetrate regardless of any defensive wall. They are too powerful and sometimes dangerously camouflaged in the appearance of everyday events. Then what else can we do? This brings us to the area of emotional resilience. By mastering appropriate psycho-physiological techniques we can build our emotional resilience to such a level that even the most challenging of threats can be rebuffed without harm to health or performance. This sounds a bit grand and too good to be true so we need to have a closer look.

There are a range of techniques available which broadly follow the same principles. Typically, these interventions are relaxation or meditation techniques centred initially on awareness of our breathing. Why breathing? Because it is a natural body rhythm requiring no conscious input. It is therefore a way of bypassing the thinking brain where we may be experiencing all sorts of activity and clutter. This approach takes us via the lungs directly to the heart. As we become more attuned to our breathing our minds will gradually relax and our hearts will take over. The cortex and limbic layers can ease down as there is no imminent threat and the response of the body is largely autonomic, requiring no new instructions.

Having accessed the first level of relaxation, the second step usually entails introducing an imagined positive personal experience into the exercise. This is done by remembering or picturing a special event or person in our lives when we felt loved and valued, one where we experienced a deep sense of peace. For those more spiritually inclined this could be a higher presence. At this point we are supporting the brain to access positive internal references. Fundamentally, we feel good and the better we get at doing this, the deeper our sense of well-being will be.

This is the essence of meditation and, whilst sometimes used for spiritual purposes, the results are compelling in terms of emotional and physical health. And do not underestimate the potential here in terms of power and clarity of thought. As you relax into such a regime, slowly your thoughts can become disentangled and, with practice, you will allow room for fresh light and insight; breakthroughs can come at the least expected time.

The classic example here is Buddhist monks. Until recent times, these monks have been inaccessible to science but the current Dalai Lama has changed this. The strength of his belief means that he is not threatened by scientific exploration; instead he embraces it. Unlike his predecessors, he has been happy for his monks to work with scientists in areas such as the development of the mind. His approach is that he has his beliefs and these will remain unless science shows him that he is wrong. This wonderful state of openness has led to a level of collaboration between religion and science which is quite inspiring.

The relevance here is that Buddhist monks have subjected themselves to laboratory research to understand the power and functioning of their minds. They are important subjects because of the time and dedication they have devoted to meditation. These monks can spend up to seven hours a day meditating on the state of their humanity and spirituality. When it comes to visualisation and focus these people are well ahead of the field. Laboratory results have provided conclusive evidence of this. Not only were they able to sustain concentration for periods well beyond the norm but the strength and consistency of the electrical output from their hearts throughout the experiments was also remarkable, showing physiological evidence of extreme cardiac health and profound emotional stability.

You only have to meet a Buddhist monk to see the informal evidence for yourself: the immediate impact of their natural grace and warmth and their smiling, reassuring faces is a pleasure to behold. The monks themselves describe the meditation experience as looking out over a calm ocean on a beautiful day. Some thoughts may pass like birds flying across the horizon and quickly disappear but they will not disturb the calm of the ocean or the ultimate feeling of peace.

Back in our western world of hustle and bustle, these meditation-like experiences are often seen to be impractical or viewed with scepticism. For many of us this is a missed opportunity. Instead, we have seen a growth in the awareness and practice of mindfulness. Now a very popular subject in current literature, mindfulness is built on similar principles. By quietening the rushing mind, such as focusing on an entirely natural process as our breathing, we can learn to settle into a deeper personal space where we are able to observe our thoughts and sense our feelings without being carried away by them. This can lead to a deeper understanding of our own personal inner dynamics and a feeling of being at one with our environment.

In brain terms, mindfulness practice enables at least two things to happen. Firstly, the natural flow of the experience allows our intuitive intelligence to surface; secondly, we allow the pre-frontal cortex to operate as the moderator of the active mind. The combined effect is to clear the cognitive clutter to allow the deeper personal light to shine from within – the place where intuition meets inner awareness. These deeper insights seem to come to us spontaneously. We have not forced our thinking process, yet in calming the mind we appear to discover a new level of intelligence. We learn to calm the stormy waters of the thinking and the emotional currents to discover an ocean of peacefulness, and in this state of accentuated sensory awareness we can experience a depth of feeling and a powerful simplicity of insights that was previously hidden.

In practical terms, more and more people are turning to mindfulness as a means of reducing anxiety and regaining a level of emotional control of their lives. It can bring with it a much greater sense of what is going on around us and how we are responding to these triggers. In this sense, it is giving the pre-frontal cortex a better chance of moderating our experiences as we hold our awareness for a longer period in working memory. Practised effectively over a longer period of time, this will build greater self-awareness and stronger emotional resilience. We may be a long way from becoming Buddhist monks but we may at least share some small steps in their journey.

ONGOING HEALTH

Of course, we are not in total control when it comes to determining our own health. Genetics will always play its part, whether it is hereditary health or disease. Despite this, there is huge value in looking after ourselves as best we can both physically and emotionally. It is a matter of positively influencing the odds. The better shape we are in, the stronger we are to respond to life's challenges.

Central to this is looking after our hearts. The heart is the engine room of the body, supplying energy, oxygen and all the nutrients essential for cell health and function. When illness threatens it is the heart that will send out the defence troops to ward off the attack and to recover the damage. It will do its best to look after us, so what are we doing to look after it? Pursuing a life of inactivity and emotional abuse feels to me like breaking a promise, the 'promise of life', the 'contract' between heart and brain to work together to give us a life of purpose.

And let's not forget the brain. It too deserves to be treated well. Aerobic exercise and emotional stability are gifts to the brain and, especially in later life, regular stimulation will keep the currents flowing and the wheels turning. Brain plasticity, as discussed earlier, is a mechanism of constant neural repair, replacement and reinvention. Like the heart, it will do all it can to keep us meaningfully engaged in our environments. Appreciating its gift to us is a great mantra for inner peace.

SECTION 4:
PERFORMANCE AND LEADERSHIP

"First say to yourself what you would be;
and then do what you have to do."

- Epictetus

In this section we will look at this subject matter both within an organisational and sporting context.

CHAPTER 4.1:

Elite Performance

Ever since I was young I have been fascinated by human performance and what makes some of us excel while others struggle. In this chapter we will explore advanced human performance and areas such as personal confidence.

What is it that makes certain people take their chosen performance areas to such high levels of attainment, whether it is sport, occupational careers or artistic excellence, such as musicianship? Firstly, we need to look at this from a physiological perspective. Of course, there are many physical considerations which will predetermine to some degree the areas we are likely to excel in. In sport, major physical attributes such as height, muscle, speed and strength will be great advantages for contact sports; lighter frames and aerobic capacity will be valuable for endurance activities. Dexterity will be a prerequisite for most musical tasks. The physical attributes for organisational success are less clear.

Yet I am less concerned here with what is observable from the outside, where we are largely in the hands of genetics and performance development regimes. Instead I am more interested in what is happening on the inside; this is where neuroscience can offer us some fascinating insights.

If successful performance was simply about physical or intellectual attributes, application skills, training and execution, the best would always thrive and the worst would always suffer. Sporting contests would be pretty meaningless affairs as results would always be predictable. Yet the sporting world itself is a perfect example of just how invalid this assumption would be. Of course, there are broadly distinguishable levels of skills, such as professionals and amateurs, but the passion of sport itself revolves around the uncertainty of the results. As competitors and fans alike we put ourselves through varying degrees of emotional trauma simply for the opportunity to experience success over our rivals, to share in the moment of self and peer recognition. In organisations, why are we 'up for it' sometimes then at other times our performance suffers? Why is human performance not a predictable mechanistic process? Why can't we be calibrated like factory machines for ongoing optimum performance?

A significant factor in answering this question revolves around the role played by our emotions. Our emotional state will play a huge part in whether we are able to stay focused on performing or whether we are overtaken by the fear of failure.

The significance of the emotional aspect of performance started to gain fresh insight with the work of Daniel Goleman in his ground-breaking book *Emotional Intelligence* originally published in 1995. In this book Goleman cited research carried out to compare the performance of graduates with high intellectual quotas (IQ) with the general population of graduates. This looked at how well each group had progressed in their chosen careers. The standard assumption at the time would have been that those with the greater intellectual power would outperform the wider graduate group but the results showed no significant difference. The proposition that emerged from this is that emotional intelligence is equally important in determining how successful we will be in realising our ambitions. Emotional intelligence here would have included the ability to connect meaningfully with our peers, to be able to influence and build relationships and to work effectively within teams.

Today, this conclusion might appear more self-evident as awareness of emotional intelligence has become more widespread, although in my experience there is still a lot more emphasis in many organisations and educational establishments on intellectual prowess and development than on their emotional equivalents. Nevertheless, Goleman's work laid the platform for others to build on and some important progress has been made.

My own experience has included working with professional sportspeople and teams, mainly in football and golf. I recall having many discussions with players in the dressing rooms about the difference between 'form' and 'talent'. Footballers themselves would turn up for every game with pretty much the same skill-set, knowledge, fitness level and ambition as the previous game, so why could they play well one week and then see their 'form' take a dip in the next match? This is where we explored how critical it was to manage our emotions effectively.

The lesson was that one of the biggest factors of all is how we *feel* about the challenge we are undertaking. This has little to do with objective analysis or tactical considerations but is instead the internal state of our emotional systems. If we feel positive about the task we face, whether sporting or organisational, our emotional system will support achievement of the targeted outcome, no energy is wasted on distractions and we will go about the task with conviction. On the other hand, if we don't feel good about the task we will trigger fear reactions in the body which will destroy concentration and waste energy in the pursuit of internalised threats.

Emotions are always targeted, so the real question is what are we targeting our emotions on? If we are internally signalling threats and thoughts of failure then that is what our emotions will target as they seek to address the threat. If we are targeting a positive outcome, not only will our hormonal mix change (such as from cortisol to dopamine) but also our emotions will align behind achievement of the goal. In my own experience, in immediate preparation for matches we would spend important time for the players to reconnect emotionally with their natural talents and ambitions. Going on to the pitch fearing failure and dejection is a recipe for poor performance, whereas feeling good about the game gives us the best chance of success.

Of course, these principles apply whatever performance challenge we are facing, whether it is a presentation we have to do to a room full of strangers or a delicate operation we have to undertake where the consequences of failure are high. These insights have great significance for those in leadership roles, a theme we shall explore further in the next chapter.

So, if we accept the logic of this, why isn't it just a case of learning to think positively? Surely the desired results would follow? Regrettably, it is not as easy as this, as anyone who has tried unsuccessfully to control their nerves under pressure will tell you. The key word here is *think*. Thinking positively is not enough. Thinking alone does not convince our emotional system. As I explained earlier, emotions have the power to override our thoughts but thoughts do not have the power to override our emotions. So, no matter how good our analysis and cognitive preparation, if we are still holding fears of failure, they will burst through our rational dam when the pressure increases and our mental preparation process will be washed away in the currents of emotional negativity.

I recall standing at the first hole of a professional golfing tournament looking at what top level players face when they go off the first tee.

For most of us mere mortals the picture is terrifying: hundreds of people lined up on either side of the projected shot eager to press forward and to be impressed by what they were about to witness. Despite my apparent personal awareness of what the brain has to do to cope with this, I felt anxious. If it was me taking the shot all I would be thinking about is, firstly, not hitting anyone with my ball and becoming the first golfer to kill somebody on a live televised golf tournament and, secondly, just wanting to get off the tee as quickly as possible to avoid the threat of embarrassment and exposure. Thankfully, it wasn't me who had to take the shot!

There is a serious observation here, even if it at first appears obvious. The difference between a professional golfer and me is that the professional trusts himself or herself to perform the required task. Effective execution depends significantly on the degree to which we trust ourselves, whether we believe we have the required capabilities to undertake the task required. Self-trust of this sort does not come through simply thinking it through; it needs to feel like it is a part of us, something that we have practised for so long that we do not have to think about it. It has become instinctive. In everyday language it has become hard-wired into our brains. When we are executing at the instinctive level we are bypassing our emotions. The emotional joker of the pack is therefore removed and the game can continue without emotional unknowns.

This last scenario also leads us into the next critical factor, which is that of visual imagery. If we cannot see or envisage something then we cannot believe it and if we cannot believe it we cannot achieve it. Being able to connect with an inner vision acts as an emotional rehearsal for the brain; it gives us a sense of direction by enabling us to visualise the path we take. This is of fundamental importance to our state of self-trust and belief. We spend more than six times the amount of energy internally processing images as opposed to processing images from the outside world. Images sit at the heart of our memory and our instinctive responses. We seek a visual reference to guide us. If we can see the required outcome in our mind's eye we have a chance of achieving it. If we do not see this we have nothing to believe in.

Visualisation has become a critical part of elite performance in sport. Athletes of all types need to be able to visualise what success looks like. If they can picture a successful outcome their brains at least know what is being asked of them and understand the direction of travel. Then comes the challenge of belief! Seeing is the first step, but do we believe? Does this image represent a place where we belong? Is it a place where we personally can thrive?

If we are creating positive images of success then we are giving ourselves the best chance, but remember these are our own internal images that nobody else can share on the same level. They are not images designed to present to the world, they are an essential part of our own inner belief system. We can try to fool others but false images won't fool our own emotional system. If we create images of failure, typically as a response to pressure and anxiety, then the internal references we are using are negative and defeatist. We are inadvertently telling the brain what failure looks like rather than success and failure is the path we will follow.

Of course, we know from practical experience that even the clearest visualisation and the deepest belief do not guarantee success. There are environmental factors to consider; our own talents may not be good enough; and, in a competitive environment, no matter how well we have performed against our own standards, our rival may still be better than us. So the key to performance success cannot be guaranteed by a magical concoction of talent, vision, emotional stability and belief, but we can guarantee that ultimate performance success will not be achieved if any one of them is missing.

THE ZONE

A term which has become popular in the sporting media is the 'zone'. This represents an episode of peak performance, when we are able to maintain a standard of execution which sits well above our personal norms. It is worth us looking at this in more depth from a neurophysiological perspective.

The physiological essence of being in the zone is the state of entrainment we described in an earlier chapter. It exists when the heart has stepped up to the role of conductor of the body's neurological orchestra. The electromagnetic rhythm of the heart transmits energy waves which entrain the other key players (especially the heart and the gut) to align behind one common purpose. This is a state of optimal arousal where the correlation between our levels of adrenaline and our performance is most productive. Too much adrenaline and we become overexcited, waste energy and become too easily distracted; too little and we are lethargic and lack attention.

The zone can be described as a calm state of concentration and spontaneous performance, a state which can only happen when the mind is at one with the body. It can be experienced as an exhilarating sense of purpose and total immersion in the task, when our senses are optimised and our instincts are positively engaged. It is a glimpse of our absolute potential.

This may not be easy to recognise, but just think of occasions when you have been at your absolute best, when you have taken on a task and proven your ability to excel. The experience in the moment is one of direct connection with our environment, where we are sensing rather than thinking and simply doing rather than analysing. Self-consciousness drops away as we become at one with the task. It is the time when we can both experience and reveal our true capability.

In my own life I can readily think of a particular occasion when I felt I was unequivocally in the zone. This was when I played cricket at a semi-professional level and was batting against two very fast bowlers. Conditions were quite dark and other batsmen were being dismissed very quickly by the speedsters, yet for some reason on that day I was able to deal with anything they threw at me. I could see the ball as if it were a football and the speed of my reflexes kept me protected from the sometimes violent assault. I scored a lot of runs and undoubtedly look back on this as the best batting performance of my life. It felt effortless, as though I was completely in tune with the environment and my own capability to cope with it. I was totally in flow. But this wasn't just a good performance, it was literally exceptional, so exceptional indeed that I could never repeat it again!

The zone is the word usually used when we can execute or witness an exceptional performance outcome, when we are able to see the precision of the golfer or the majesty of the tennis player. Yet it also describes a more common experience, that of the sensation of confidence. It may not always be associated with a visible outcome that attracts public attention, it is something which can happen on a daily basis, when we enter a state of quiet conviction and know in the moment that we are where we belong and are perfectly suited to executing the task. This could be as subtle as making a point of debate over dinner to delivering a presentation to a large crowd; there is a feeling of inner calm that makes us feel we have got it right.

In Chapter 3.4 I described resilience as a feature of the physiological state of entrainment. The same is true for confidence, although whilst we tend to think of resilience as an ongoing state, we know that confidence is something that can elude in a single moment. Nevertheless, confidence is the energetic state of alignment between mind and body or, more precisely, when the heart entrains the wider neurological system, including the brain and gut. In this state our energy and attention are optimised, our senses are attuned and our conviction is one of quiet calm that we can achieve. In human terms, the essential ingredient is belief.

COMPETITIVE INSTINCTS

I would argue that the desire to perform is a fundamental evolutionary instinct. At the simplest level mammals seek to learn by mirroring. They then discard the practices that don't work and instead seek to perfect those that do. By constant experimentation and practical execution they fine-tune their skills and thereby enhance their opportunity for survival and energy optimisation. In the same way, humans are drawn to opportunities to thrive. When we sense an environmental opportunity to advance, our instinctive response will be to grab it with both hands.

Sustainable survival itself depends on seizing opportunities to advance. For reptiles this could be as rudimentary as recognising the environmental conditions that are best suited to making the next kill. For mammals there will also be driving factors concerned with strengthening their place in the social hierarchy. Why else would maturing gorillas risk their lives to confront the existing alpha male who sits at the head of the group? As humans, we are driven by factors other than those essential to survival or immediate social standing. Part of the human essence is our own very deep and personal search for meaning and fulfilment. As the only species with an advanced pre-frontal cortex, humans alone have both the opportunity and the burden to reflect on who we are and why we are here. Whilst we are likely to enjoy the recognition of our achievements by our peers, there is nothing so compelling as to prove our value to the one who seeks to understand it the most – ourselves!

Imagine an environment which offered no feedback on anything we did or said. This is the scenario of screaming in space, where nobody can hear us. It is a fundamental human need to put ourselves 'out there' by word or deed and to build our understanding of the impact we create. If there is no evidence of impact, who are we? Surely that makes us nothing? But we can't cope with this concept of nothingness. Our brain does not 'do' nothing, it can only process data about *something.* As such we are programmed to constantly seek validation of our impact on our world and those around us. We cannot survive in an emotional vacuum. It therefore follows that when significant opportunities present themselves to really make our mark, the personal drive in us becomes compelling. Our fundamental concept of self is based on this principle, and with it comes our own perspective of self-value.

The drive for advanced human performance is therefore an ongoing instinctive, and therefore obligatory, quest to establish who we are in a way that validates us to ourselves and provides us with meaning at the deepest personal level.

It is also self-evident that humans are competitors with other species in the battle for survival. The essential basis of the 'survival of the fittest' is that not everyone can be a winner in the competition for scarce resources. The evolutionary journey so far has been littered with winners and losers. This competitive instinct remains with us today, for better or worse, and sits deep at the heart of our quest for superior performance.

GAINING MASTERY

So how do we achieve mastery in our chosen area? Mastery itself is a relative term as we can only really assess it against the performance of others. To excel in any field it is inevitable that we need to show dedication and commitment to learning the skills and knowledge required. Malcom Gladwell has commented extensively on the 10,000 hours typically needed to perfect a complex skill, whether musician, sportsman or other technical practitioner. But what does this mean in terms of the brain?

Perfection of a skill first necessitates an understanding of the task and the skills required for execution. This is where the cortex is engaged in conscious analysis of these needs and establishing the rules of execution. Then comes experimentation. We need to play with the challenge, to handle the tools and get into physical skill development. Now we are engaging the unconscious regions of the brain, which are both the limbic and basal systems, to use our sensory intelligence to engage our motor neural skills to effect precise movement. Initially, progress will be clunky and execution will feel mechanical. It is a frequent occurrence to see those learning golf focusing so much on the technicalities of the game, such as their position and swing, that they momentarily switch off from the more natural talents of judgement of pace and distance. This is inevitable.

Slowly and surely, through practice, the task should become easier and we need to spend less time analysing and more time just doing. In this case, the unconscious system works like a missile guidance system: once the requirements of the task are understood, the brain will lock on to the target and constantly refine its application. Over time the relevant neural connections become myelin encased, thereby strengthening the links and 'fast-tracking' execution. This is when we can execute the task without really thinking about it.

Recall when you learnt to drive a motor car. The process was clumsy and frustrating at first and full of errors; now you can drive home from work and find yourself arriving at your home hardly recalling what the journey involved along the way. Think about the layout of your computer keyboard; if you were asked to draw a diagram of the exact location of each key my guess is you would find it an arduous task. Yet observe your own speed of use of the keyboard. In the more accomplished amongst us it is as though our fingers can sense the letters before our brains can work out consciously where they are. This is mastery in action.

Tim Gallwey's book *The Inner Game of Tennis* takes this explanation of mastery to another level. In particular, he warns against the dangers of losing touch with our natural talents as we embark on intensive training and skill development programmes. Of course, attaining a level of technical excellence is essential but overdoing the conscious mechanics of learning a skill will not give us the best result. Overthinking means too much dependence on the cortex, the slowest part of the brain when it comes to responding to the external environment. Importantly we must retain a balance. The sensory and instinctive abilities of the brain will serve us well if we allow them to engage naturally. Responding to the unpredictable bounce of a ball coming at you at speed on the tennis court is a skill which our unconscious system is far more equipped to cope with than our conscious system.

Mastery is therefore about putting in the hours of dedication needed to attain the technical learning of the skill; thereafter it is about learning to trust our senses and instincts at the point of execution. Our senses will keep us attuned to the demands of the immediate environment and sense what is needed and our instinctive abilities will give us the capability to respond. In a paraphrase of Gallwey's words: "If your body knows how to do something let it happen, if it doesn't let it learn."

For me, learning to work with our instincts is likely to be a far more productive route than, for instance, repeating mantras. I can understand how repeating a positive statement may have some effect on mindset, but the words of the mantra alone achieve very little. For many, the repeating of a mantra is a form of cognitive self-persuasion; the problem arises when it is based primarily in thought alone and where it lacks emotional or spiritual connection.

When the pressure is on, emotions will invade and displace our thoughts and the mantra can be set aside as an item on a wish list.

For others, the mantra represents an association with faith and beliefs. In this case, the exercise is likely to be more beneficial, as the associative links trigger a deeper sense of inner peace. Emotional resilience is a far stronger platform to build on than cognitive resilience.

In the same way, overanalysing a task at the point of execution takes us into a state of self- awareness but this is not the best state for performance excellence. Of course, we need to think about the way that tasks have been performed in the past and how they might be performed in the future, but excellent performance is about *being* in the moment, not thinking about it or worrying about it. 'Being' implies a total immersion in the task, calling on all our senses and instincts to perfect the execution. It is interesting to experience the dissipation of ego when we are truly in the zone. Our normal boundaries of self-awareness disappear and are replaced by a feeling of oneness with our environment. We are in flow, there is minimal sense of personal boundaries. Performance becomes a natural function of our being. When we lack confidence, we become very self-aware and retreat into a cocoon of self-doubt, negative images flood the brain and successful execution becomes virtually impossible.

CHAPTER 4.2:

Leadership: Energy and Vision

*"A dream you dream alone is only a dream.
A dream you dream together is reality."*

– John Lennon

In this next section I would like to look at a very specific form of performance, that of leadership. Having spent many years working in, or supporting, organisations in business and public services, including a role as CEO of an organisation of about 1,500 people, it is a subject that is deeply imbedded in my experience.

Since becoming aware of neuroscience in about 2005, I have been very committed to taking the value of its insights into organisations, and this has particularly involved working with leaders and their leadership teams. Over this time I have always looked for the neuroscientific perspective on any challenge that we came across. My perspective has been based on the premise that if we can understand the brain (and heart) dynamics in any given situation, we are building a refreshed knowledge base that is far more reliable that just another psychological model. Experience has also taught me that many of the insights are more radical and far-reaching. So let's now take a look at some of the areas of challenge and debate that are frequently associated with leading organisations.

A very common phrase in the corporate world relates to the requirement to win the 'hearts and minds' of those we wish to lead. I would like to offer some different words and refer instead to 'energy and vision'. It may not be as catchy but it helps better explanation.

LEADERSHIP ENERGY

We discussed energy in an earlier chapter and recognised that there is a transactional dynamic going on between us minute by minute and day by day. Our impact on each other is not just a mental process, it is also energetic. We can influence people's energy by the energetic state we project ourselves. Energy speaks directly to the heart as electromagnetic wave forms are translated by the heart and brain into emotional data. We know this; we can make people feel welcome or defensive without saying a word. Gestures, body positioning and facial expression will communicate quicker than any rational exchange.

This is the world of energetic priming we discussed earlier. It deserves to be revisited here as it is a vital part of effective leadership. Leaders who have an energising effect on their people are far more likely to get a successful response than those who drain energy or create defensive energy. If leaders go into a situation feeling tense or defeated, there is a great chance that they will create exactly the same response in their colleagues. Those who approach similar challenges with clarity and confidence are far more likely to succeed.

This is a deeper challenge than simply controlling our behaviour. We can learn to behave 'professionally' but if our feelings are transmitting negativity, our colleagues will see the behaviour as simply 'toeing the line' or 'putting on a brave face'. In these circumstances, the heart will determine what is true and the mind will follow. It follows therefore that handling our own energy as leaders is as crucial as any attempt to manage the energy of others. Yet, after all my years of experience, I am still struck by the frequency of occasions when leaders lack awareness of the energetic impact of their actions and their own disposition.

This sits at the heart of another classic corporate debate: the difference between management and leadership. In most organisations, there is a consensus that leadership is more specifically about handling people, whereas management is about ensuring tasks are carried out through those who report to us. This is fine, but it remains superficial. All too often, appointed leaders accept this distinction at a rational level and then proceed to demonstrate complete ignorance of the energetic impact they are having on their people; and, to be fair to many of them, they have had little training or education to help them develop this sensitivity.

This is not a nuance or simple irritation; it strikes at the core of organisational effectiveness. Insensitive leadership drives people into defensive behaviour, where they feel the need to put their own survival needs above those of the organisation because there is no collective trust. The term 'sensitivity' would itself not necessarily resonate well with modern corporate parlance; it smacks of being 'soft' and indecisive. Sensitivity here should not imply pampering to emotional weakness or distraction; it should represent a true awareness of people dynamics and how they can be best influenced to achieve successful outcomes.

It is striking to me how people will sometimes 'judge' a word before they commit to really understanding it. I can understand this, certain words will trigger an associative meaning which we may find to be disturbing. If previous bosses of ours have constantly sniped against the 'weakness' of words such as sensitivity, our conditioned response is likely to be dismissive. Here we must be wary of our own immediate behaviour and our own tendency to judge when the truth may appear uncomfortable. Judgement denies us the better choices that might be available for how we handle the future.

The result of insensitive leadership is a constant undercurrent of misalignment and tension. The cost of this conflict, if measured, would feature in big red numbers in any profit and loss statement or balance sheet. It is unfortunate for business as a whole that today we do not have the accounting or human resource methodologies to expose the true cost of these missed opportunities, although my guess is that some organisations would prefer it to stay that way.

Effective leadership is also a function of how we manage our own energy. In this context we often hear references to good leaders having 'gravitas', so what is this? People who are seen to have gravitas are people who have learnt (probably intuitively) to 'centre' their own energy. By understanding and trusting the internal source of our own energy (alignment between heart and brain) we transmit energy rather than take it from others. We therefore become a source of energy supply and others in our presence will sense this and tap into it. In this state we are transmitting a strong electromagnetic signal and group engagement can amplify this effect.

The common phrase 'group think' is too limited as it underplays the energetic dimension. So when groups get together and become excited it fosters a collective adrenaline effect. There is a mass energetic transfer going on which has a multiplying effect. This has little to do with logic or the simple rational alignment of minds; it is the alignment and amplification of emotions.

We see this on a regular basis at sports games. Any professional athlete will testify to the power of the crowd and how their energetic mood can directly impact the players. The whole basis of home advantage in sports games is based on this principle. On a more sinister level we have seen group energy take over when lynch mobs are activated. In this highly aroused environment, rationality goes out of the window; it can only attempt to sort out the mess afterwards but the damage has often already been done.

So, being attuned to human energy dynamics is a critical competence for the effective leader. This will position the leader to gauge the mood and be able to respond in an informed way. It is also a prerequisite for building key relationships across the business. Leaders cannot themselves build relationships between other people but they can foster a culture which recognises the importance of relationships and ensures that accountability for their success is an organisational driver. I find it curious that some organisations have 'relationship managers' offering a service to customers but no such function exists for internal purposes. Internal relationships appear to be a game of chance: you are lucky if you have a good manager or leader and unlucky if you don't. It appears that effective internal relationships are sometimes considered a bonus rather than an essential platform for organisational success. How can this make sense when we know that emotions are the prime driver of our organisational experience and relationships are, in turn, the prime driver of our emotional exchanges?

There is ample evidence to show the correlation between team relationships and performance. Teams who enjoy working with each other are invariably more effective than teams who don't. Of course, some level of success may well be achieved without a strong relationship base; strong individuals in teams may ensure a level of success in their own territories, but this is not team optimisation. Much of the corporate world has been seduced by the apparent need for tough and decisive leaders who can be relied upon to get things done. Indeed there is little doubt that strength and decisiveness are vital ingredients to performance. The problem arises when this is only achieved at the 'silo' level. Strong leaders are often instinctively territorial and concerned primarily with the performance of their own area. As a result, the only person working for the good of the whole can be the team boss, the CEO.

Again, here we have to be fair to these so-called 'silo-leaders'. Their careers to date have typically been built on exactly the principles we may now be trying to set aside. In environments which have created, by intent or default, a culture of 'every man for himself', it is not surprising that those who have thrived the most to get to the top of their pile will hang on to the lessons and behaviours they have learnt to get them there. Add to this the divisive nature of so many business incentive schemes which reward individual performance over team performance, then it is hardly surprising that top team behaviour can sometimes more resemble a political carve-up than a team collective.

I have had some exposure to professional sports teams and there is no greater diagnostic than sensing what is going on in the team dressing room. Yes, we can see the ultimate performance of sports teams when they enter the field of play. The results will speak for themselves and there exists in most professional sport a brutal commitment to the demands of being in a results-based business. Yet the point is often missed that the platform for successful performance on the field is built off the field. On the training ground it is about tactics, stamina and skills; in the dressing room it is about relationships. Do the players in the team really want to work with each other? Do they know and trust each other? Do they understand each other's behaviour so well that they feel they can rely on the support of the rest of the team even without thinking about it? A dressing room that is split, or dominated by one or two individuals, or lacking collective energy and trust, is one that will not set the team up for optimum performance. Relationships will be carried on to the field of play and can either strengthen or weaken team performance. The field of play should be a performance arena, where learnt skills are executed in an instinctive and confident state of mind; relationships have to be built in advance.

It is worthwhile for any organisational leader to reflect on when their team is 'in play' and when it is in preparation. This may seem strange as the team does not typically disband and recreate. Yet the team is not always in play as a team. The irony for me is that so many teams seem to think they are in play only when they meet and the rest of the time they go back to being individuals. I would argue that this needs to be flipped on its head. Much time spent in leadership team meetings should be seen as the practice or training ground. Yes, there are important elements when the team needs to make decisions or take positions, but there is also a lot of time spent simply catching up with each other and sharing perspectives. Nothing wrong with this but my worry is that the distinction between training ground and field of play gets blurred.

Surely the field of play for a leadership team is the arena in which they lead – this means their organisation. In many team sports we talk about 'crossing the white line', which refers to the point of entry to the field of play when all that matters is the performance that follows and the result that is achieved. When does a leadership team cross the white line? It has to be the moment they leave the team meeting and re-enter their own field of play, which means the point at which they step back into leading their own part of the organisation. This also means that they need to see themselves as the representative of the whole team before they see themselves as the boss of their own particular territory.

Unfortunately, current perceptions do not support this argument. In most organisations there is little sustained awareness of, or belief in, team leadership across a total organisation. The focus instead is on individual and hierarchical accountability. We are trapped in an organisational Catch 22: there is no expectation of collective team leadership as no one has experienced it, and because it has never been seriously explored, there is no belief in it. It remains a 'nice conversation', confined to the team meeting room, never to breathe the air beyond the office walls.

MEASURING ORGANISATIONAL ENERGY

It is clear to me, based on my leadership experience, that organisational energy needs to be measured in a business to keep it visible on the leadership agenda. This is effectively cultural data and the stuff of employee surveys. Top teams need the cultural equivalent of the trading P&L (profit and loss statement) to give them evidence of cultural state and trends. Whereas the P&L measures the output of a business, it can reasonably be argued that employee surveys measure the human input, at least in energetic terms. Make no mistake, the impact of a morale problem in a business will find its way on to the P&L, you just won't be able to isolate it.

The problem with the traditional approach to employee surveys is that they have been too infrequent and ponderous. By the time data is collected and analysed, the issue has moved on. Fortunately, the technology is now available to measure and analyse such data on an immediate and regular basis. Leadership teams need to have their fingers on the pulse of the flow of energy within their business and they need the reliability and tangibility of measurement data to back it up.

LEADERSHIP VISION

So the management of organisational energy, emotions and relationships is a fundamental dimension of successful leadership. There is another area of equal importance, that of Vision.

There is much business school literature on the need for organisations to have a business vision. I agree with this need but, in most cases, I don't agree with the way it is approached. My own neuroscience perspective leads me to see a vision in this context as a vital ingredient to connect with the instinctive brain, but this part of the brain does not do detail. Vision statements that drift into detailed commentaries have missed the point when it comes to leadership. A vision should be what it says on the can: it should be visual!

The leadership challenge in this case is about creating a vision or image in the brains of those we choose to lead, one which they can relate to and identify with. It is an instant reference point that ideally gives them both direction and purpose. If it is detailed, the instinctive brain will get bored very quickly and leave it to the cortex to sift through. The problem is that the cortex seeks clarity but it is not the source of motivation. Motivation is best triggered at the instinctive level when we can sense an opportunity to thrive. Think back to the crocodile we described in the early stages of the book: an effective vision enables us to picture ourselves in a place that feels right for us; it gives us that sense of where we belong, an environment that suits our evolutionary purpose.

If we cannot see something in our minds, we cannot follow it. Being able to visualise an environment acts as a rehearsal for the emotional and behavioural journey that lies ahead. It allows us to focus our internal resources. We have to be able to see ourselves there; if we cannot it is motivationally irrelevant.

Communicating a vision does not necessarily mean showing a picture, although any visual support is welcome. Words can be very powerful in evoking images. This may seem a contradiction as language is really the domain of the cortex. It is not the words themselves but more the images they can trigger if presented effectively and delivered with energy. Take the oratory prowess of historic figures like Winston Churchill and Doctor Martin Luther King.

My parents often related to me the importance they attached to the speeches of Churchill during the Second World War, especially in the 1940/1 period when the threat of invasion seemed imminent. There was no television, so families would huddle together around their wirelesses waiting for news. When Churchill spoke to the nation they clung on to every word because, above all, the one thing they needed most in those dark days was hope. In the "we will fight them on the beaches" speech, Churchill painted a picture of defiance and belief that this nation would "never surrender". Creating such a powerful shared image in the minds of those he led offered them a meaningful connection with a prospect for survival. When our instincts are positively engaged our emotions will respond and we will find energy to support the cause.

We can also see the parallels with Doctor Martin Luther King. His "I have a dream" speech is the perfect example of painting a leadership vision: no detail, no facts and figures, no hows and whats, just a picture of hope that connected his audience with their burning sense of injustice and enabled them to see how their struggle could be won. If people cannot visualise a destiny they do not know which path to follow. They need to know what success looks like.

CHAPTER 4.3:

Organisational Practices

"Besides the noble art of getting things done, there is the noble art of leaving things undone.

The wisdom of life consists in the elimination of non-essentials."

– Lin Yutang

There are other neuroscientific insights which are relevant for organisational practice, some of which we can examine here.

BRAND

A good place to start is to refresh our view of company brand. Businesses spend huge amounts of money promoting their brands but they usually have not looked significantly to any psychological understanding to support this. They do it because it works. It is self-evident that there is no point in having a great product if nobody knows about it, but the world of branding is about so much more than recognition levels. Our reaction to brand perception again demonstrates the power of the unconscious mind.

Brand is all about association: it is the instantaneous reaction triggered by the brand stimulus. When we perceive a recognised brand we immediately match it with the memory held in our emotional system and react accordingly. If the associative memory is positive, we are immediately predisposed to view it in a favourable way. Likewise, if the memory is negative our initial response will be unfavourable. Rational reasoning may follow but the lingering impact of the initial association does have a significant influence on whether objectivity even comes into the equation. A company's brand, usually presented by some visual logo, is a distilled encapsulation of all that the company represents. As potential consumers we register that brand in a split second and may find it very hard to shake off. Companies who neglect their brand have little prospect of sustainable survival.

SELLING

The ability to sell is critical to the success of any business organisation. Whilst having a good product or proposition is important, success can still be substantially influenced by the skill of the sales person. Yet I still have to endure being sold to on a regular basis, whether it is unwelcome cold calls or having to listen to the next PowerPoint presentation slavishly rolled out at a business meeting. So what is the neuroscience angle on this? It can only tell us what the good salesperson already knows: selling is primarily about relationships. 'People buy from people' is a common mantra in sales circles but it is still easy to see many examples of selling approached as a purely transactional process.

Whilst it is generally reasonable to presume that none of us will willingly buy something we don't want or need, when we do buy, the relationship with the salesperson we encounter is critical. If he creates a relationship with us (albeit temporary) our brain will be in engagement mode and we will be open to a purchase. If we distrust him, the possibility of a sale will be significantly reduced.

Selling is as much about managing the energy of an interpersonal exchange as it is about commercial reality. If the salesperson creates a 'push' energy (being 'in your face' or being locked into a transactional selling methodology), the likely effect is indeed to push the potential purchaser away. The brain is best persuaded when it is not aware that it is being sold to. A sense of the salesperson's agenda only creates a level of survival response in us and we back off from engagement. If he connects with us at the human level we are far more likely to open our minds to be persuaded because it is built on a level of trust.

The same principles apply when there is no salesperson directly involved, such as in consumer retail. This is where brand comes into play. Brand (as discussed earlier) is the virtual salesperson who has the potential to create the right emotional association for the purchase to proceed.

LEARNING

Neuroscience has also thrown up some interesting insights into the way we learn. Organisations often talk about creating a learning culture, an ambition I would totally encourage. Yet, to be more precise, we should be aiming for a 'learning and teaching' culture. The brain learns best when it knows what it is expected to do with the information it is receiving. In this way we create internal images of the scenario when we are using the information. This gives us a sense of application purpose and our attention will become more active and effective.

There has been important research in the USA to back this up, particularly within the education system. Students who were told in advance that they would be required to teach the information they received to another set of students learnt the information much better than those who were simply learning for their own sake.

This insight can be extended to the wider issue of organisational learning. Most corporate organisations remain over-reliant on the classroom when it comes to behavioural training. Typically, employees are taken out of their normal working environment to a central learning centre to be educated in new techniques and knowledge. This is understandable considering the logistics and availability of centralised teaching competence, but all too often it does not work. The biggest challenge for most learning within organisations is not what is understood in the classroom but more how to apply it in the working environment. When trainees return to their normal operational environments, ideally informed and enthused, their colleagues have not been on the same programme and will carry on behaving the way they always have. If the learning they have just received is not kept alive by daily experience, it will wither and die and we remain stuck with the status quo.

To be fair, this is already recognised in the training industry and the '70-20-10' quote is often aired, recognising that 70% of effective learning takes place while doing the job, 20% is learnt through others, and 10% in the classroom. Yet an examination of training practice still shows a significant reliance on centralised learning. In my opinion, this needs to be fundamentally reversed so that front-line learning sets become a feature of all organisations and allow employees to learn as part of their normal working practice with educational support being made available at the time it is most needed.

Of course, this will throw up a significant resourcing challenge but is manageable with a change of mindset. Training competence needs to be viewed much wider than the role of central experts. People throughout the organisation have a lot to offer in supporting learning. Building on the insight discussed above, by calling on more of us to teach not only will we be better learners ourselves but our students will also be taught more effectively.

Once again, research in the USA has shown the benefits of mentoring. Pilots have shown that using older students to mentor younger students has been very successful. There is a natural opportunity for practical connection and empathy that the traditional teacher may find hard to replicate. The same principle applies in organisations. Internal mentoring and coaching can tap into the latent teaching talent in many of us, at the same time strengthening relationships at the point of application. Central educational experts can then focus less on content education and more on developing the skills and knowledge of the mentors and coaches they have across the organisation. This would truly resemble a learning organisation.

BOSSES AND RELATIONSHIPS

I have also observed some curious ongoing practices when it comes to the recruitment and selection of managers and leaders. There remains a curious attachment to macho managers who exert overt strength and decisiveness. Of course, these are attractive competences but they can come in many guises. Research shows a direct contradiction between the bosses we would like to work for and those we often appoint. When we reflect on our ideal bosses we typically think of someone with good relationship and listening skills, someone who will be fair and consistent, and a person we can trust. Yet appointment practice shows that in many cases egos win the day (and here I do mean egos in the sense of self-preoccupation).

There is a curious link with the way we compare with our parental relationships. Typically, mother is cast in the role of love-giver in the upbringing of the child, whilst father is set more as the role model, upholding standards of behaviour and presentation to the outside world. Of course, we should not generalise here and it is certainly not the only model for successful parenting. Yet if we look across mammalian species we can see that it is a trait we have inherited and is still reinforced by our hormonal connection to our offspring. It seems that in the organisational world the preoccupation with the father still lingers. We continue to see bosses as authority figures rather than love-givers or nurturers. This may go a little way to explain the continued discrimination against women in more senior positions. It is as though we feel the father role model will keep us safer, the alpha male who will protect the group from attack. Yet we all also feel that without love, acknowledgement, trust and nurture we cannot give our best. Surely it is time to rebalance the equation and give mother a better shot?

FINANCIAL INCENTIVE SCHEMES

The very common practice of individualised incentive schemes does little to encourage teamwork and a collective ethic. Of course, there is room for recognition of individual effort but in many cases making the most from incentive schemes can mean asking people to do well, if necessary, at the expense of their colleagues. Recognising the individual above the team means that, when it comes to the crunch, it is OK to leave your colleagues behind as long as you achieve your own targets. This is a survival ethos of 'every man for himself'.

I suggest that closer examination will reveal many missed opportunities for better collective performance because the people concerned have been incentivised to put themselves first. Opportunities for team optimisation will be set aside if it means endangering one's own incentives opportunity. Yet it is a practice which is still largely unquestioned. Do individuals in the corporate world really operate in such individualised spheres? Are they not reliant on their colleagues for supply, support, collaboration or information exchange? Is this not like sending a football team on to the sport field and rewarding them on the basis of their individual contributions, regardless of whether it means winning or losing the game?

Any stimulus which favours the individual over the collective will reinforce the emotions and behaviour associated with survival at the expense of our colleagues. It keeps us in our own box and we look out for ourselves above anyone else. Turn this on its head and a new environment can be fostered where the team is encouraged to support each other towards excellent collective performance. This is not a 'soft' environment. Teams aspiring towards high performance will quickly recognise that every team member needs to contribute; over time they will become mutually demanding and self-moderating.

Take the armed services as an example: there are few cases where commitment to the collective is so clearly the driving force of the team. Here everyone knows that their lives can depend on the people they have around them. We constantly hear of examples where soldiers have risked their own lives to rescue or protect their colleagues. These are hugely significant acts; they bear witness to the fact that in certain environments we can set aside our own survival instincts and commit ourselves to a wider collective purpose. Such a commitment is based on a clearly understood code of values and behaviour and an ethic of trust. Surely, the ultimate judgement to be made is that of the performance of the whole, so why is so much attention paid to encouraging individuals to see themselves as someone apart from the whole? A well-supported team environment can perform collectively well above the levels of an aggregate of individuals.

CRITICAL THINKING AND DECISION MAKING

More recently I have been asked by a number of my clients about the area of critical thinking and decision making. Most organisations recognise that intellectual power is a critical ingredient of their success and are keen to make the most of the talent they have available to them. On the other hand, they have recognised the limitations of conditioned thinking, where rational methodologies are so engrained in their culture that they struggle to think 'outside of the box', to be creative or to use their gut instinct.

Anyone who has been in a position of power in an organisation will recognise that it is very difficult to rely on rational analysis alone. The objective world of facts and figures is indeed an important point of reference but leaders are often called upon to take a position in the moment, when their people are watching, when an immediate decision matters, when they need to display conviction. Uncertainty and calling for more evidence doesn't always cut it in the buzz of everyday reality.

As we discussed earlier in the book, if we feel comfortable in the immediate environment we are confronted with our instincts and intuition will kick in and give us our answer. We may call it a hunch or a gut reaction but it is in fact a deeper and uncluttered thinking process that gives us insight when we need it most. So part of the learning challenge my clients have encountered is to get their key people to learn to recognise how to connect with their own deeper intuition and the insights it can offer.

The key differentiator between purely analytical thinking and intuitive thinking is that the former comes from without but the latter comes from within. Analytical thinking is concerned with the domain of fact and objective evidence. This then normally relies on a deductive reasoning process where we start with a wide perspective of the data and systematically work our way through it, distilling the argument through some methodology until we get to a rational conclusion. Intuition relies on making an instant personal connection with the scenario we are examining. This will be based on memory and familiarity; in our minds we have recognised a broad match between what we are seeing now and what we have experienced in the past. This will then put us in a position to know what we are looking for.

So, whilst the analyst is marshalling the data, the instinctive leader can go straight to the information that matters most. She can then cut through the complexity and decide her stance in an instant. Her reasoning process is inductive rather than deductive; it expands outward from the initial insight and will survey the bigger picture rather than the detail.

So, which is best? It really is not a case of saying that one is better than the other. They are appropriate for different needs. Using our instincts and intuition are valuable in demonstrating conviction and momentum but a leader who relies on her instincts alone is running a high risk strategy as it may be a matter of time before her instincts play out as unjustified prejudices that are blind to the real evidence in front of her. A major decision-making disaster is looming on the horizon. On the other hand, organisations that become over-reliant on objective evidence run the risk of becoming ponderous and narrow in their thinking. It is inevitable that more agile organisations will pass them by. In the commercial world, many big decisions are in fact based on a projected view of the future. Facts and figures can tell us only about the past and present.

Likewise, over-dependence on formalised methodologies can be the death knell of creativity. Creativity, like intuition, comes from within. Intuition relies on connection with the instinctive or basal region of the brain, whilst creativity flows from the limbic region. The energetic flow and analogue (state sensitive) dynamic of the limbic region is the source of a wider connectivity across the brain that enables us to see patterns that we would not see when we are simply following the rules of the digital processing of the cortex. This wider connectivity, combined with a deeper subjective meaning matched in memory, empowers us to think more radically and to see more widely. Creativity is fostered by the space it needs to flow. In its purest form, there is no method and there are no rules; it is the subjective expression of an energetic sensation and will find its own way.

We also have to be very wary of exercising judgement too quickly in our assessments. When we are viewing data our brains will be constantly looking for the matches with our past experiences. When we spot an authentic match which connects with a relevant experience it can be very powerful in helping us understand the data in front of us, but we have to be very wary of our own built-in prejudices. If our early view of the data creates a sense of unease we will be instinctively tempted to exercise judgement and take a position on something being 'bad' or 'wrong'. Likewise, an early positive view can lead to a very quick judgement that something is 'good' or 'right'. The danger we face here is that we fail to see the evidence for what it really is. Early judgement means we have simply stopped listening and have corralled the data to match our own view of the world.

History has shown us that this can be a significant challenge for those with a strong, instinctive leadership style. The strength of their conviction and their decisive qualities have typically been significant factors in their rise to the top. Yet they inadvertently lose connection over time with those they need to support them. They have stopped listening and countenance the views only of those who support their position. The eventual result is isolation for the leader and rebellion amongst the followers: witness Margaret Thatcher, Winston Churchill and even Julius Caesar. The strength of conviction overplayed becomes the weakness of arrogance.

Another example of this is the pitfall of denial. When confronted with evidence of an uncomfortable truth, we can be very adept at rationalising the data to suit our current position. We select the information to support our view that the data is the problem, not us. Many a comfort is sought in the sanctity of denial but the protection is only temporary. The walls into which we retreat to evade the truth become our prison, robbing us of the freedom to engage authentically with the world outside. Those suffering with addictive illnesses are obvious examples of this. Convincing a heavy drinker that he may have an alcohol dependency problem is the key opening challenge before any route to recovery can be pursued; hence, the Alcoholics Anonymous insistence on open acknowledgement of the truth of being an alcoholic. The journey back to authentic life engagement can only start by breaking down the walls of denial.

Sustaining concentration is a challenge for most of us when it comes to making the most of our intellectual capacity. Mind-wandering is inevitable at some point and will depend greatly on the degree to which we feel engaged in the subject matter. As we have seen earlier, a meaningful context is an important factor in this as it helps us to create the internal reference scenario that gives it purpose.

Concentration is about staying in the present and not being distracted by diversions into the past or projections into the future. Our brains have all the capability we need to concentrate our attentional resources on one focal point but this has to be accompanied by a sense of the purpose of the effort and the value to be gained.

CHAPTER 4.4:

A Performance Strategy

"Obstacles are those frightful things you see when you take your mind off your goals."

– Henry Ford

Whether in organisations or in sport, I am frequently asked questions about performance strategies. Personally I don't like coming up with complex models to explain this; it has to be kept simple, but effective. A concise model is an effective way to capture and remember the learning on offer. As with most of my models, I need look no further than the human brain. In terms of performance I refer to the Podium model.

THE PODIUM

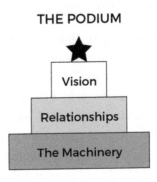

The word podium implies some acknowledgement of competitive success and can be seen rather like the medals podium at the Olympic Games. Each tier reflects the respective awards of bronze, silver and gold. They symbolise steps to success. In parallel, these tiers represent the three regions of the brain, respectively the cortex, limbic and basal regions. All three tiers have to be addressed to fulfil a high-performance strategy.

Representing the cortex, the bronze tier of the podium captures all the rational, mechanical, structural, process, procedural and data elements of the strategy. These can be regarded as the practicalities that need to be in place to support performance. In an organisation, this would include the rules of operation and the structures, processes and measures that are in place to carry them out. Think of it as the machinery and infrastructure of the organisation. In sport, this would include the systems for capturing and developing talent, such as the training regimes. It would also include the tactical plans of execution which need to be in place for tournament day.

All of these arrangements need to be fit for purpose and aligned behind the goal of the organisation or athlete. All too often performance is restricted by outdated or conflicting structures and procedures which were designed for an earlier time, yet they continue to live and breathe without dynamic evaluation and evolution. Getting the infrastructure right is vital in creating the platform for advanced performance.

Representing the limbic region, the silver tier of the podium is essentially the human emotional element, the world of feelings, relationships and energetic flow. In organisations, this would be the cultural dimension and would include people relationships and engagement dynamics. Experience has taught me just how important this is. Systems and processes can secure a minimum level of performance but they will not encourage or inspire people to give what they don't have to or want to give. Yet, so many organisations struggle with the challenge of cultural leadership. It is the end of the meeting agenda discussion that takes place after the 'serious business debate' has already taken place. In my view, culture is *the* serious business discussion but organisations so often lack the tools and techniques to bring the subject matter to the most significant audiences. Just because culture is not measured in value on the profit and loss account or the balance sheet does not mean it is not having a fundamental effect on the performance of the business. Culture needs to be led and managed as seriously and systematically as any other element of business success.

In sport, the silver tier represents the way we feel about the task we are addressing and the relationships we have with all the key stakeholders and influencers who can impact our performance. Here we come across the concept of 'form', that elusive quality that can support us so well in the good times but desert us when we most need it. My time working with athletes has reinforced how critical this is. It relates to how we feel about ourselves and those around us. It is rarely on public display but is more likely to be kept for trusted conversations with peers, friends or coaches. When we are emotionally attuned to our task we will give it our best shot and will enjoy doing so. Feeling good about what we are doing ensures energy is not wasted on negativity.

Then comes the gold tier, representing the basal region of the brain. This is the world of instinctive talent and sensory optimisation. In the sporting arena this is the concept of the 'zone' we discussed in an earlier chapter, where no energy is wasted in unnecessary analysis or emotion. It is the world of instinctive execution. We learn the rules of performance in the cortex and lay down the neural pathways necessary for execution. We practise execution of these rules in the limbic region, where we are refining internal intelligence feedback on the success or otherwise of our efforts. Once refined, instinctive execution is the domain of the basal layer, where movement and motor skills are triggered instantaneously. When a skill has been mastered we are free to go with the energetic flow of execution with the total force of our senses available to support us in the moment.

Visualisation plays a huge role in ultimate performance, as discussed earlier. In organisations, this is represented by the vision which drives it. It is vital that leadership and following connect at the visual level. Sharing a collective vison sits at the heart of effective alignment and direction. This is the place where it can all come together and is worthy of the gold award. When we have the infrastructure to support our performance and the emotional balance and fortitude to follow it through, the visual connection will engage our instinctive talents and offer them the connection and direction they need to fulfil their purpose. When the instincts are engaged, the rest will follow.

Ultimate performance comes when we pay attention and commit resources to what we love. Feeling personally fulfilled and finding the environment where we can best survive and thrive is a function of our deepest evolutionary instincts. Ultimately, human performance is a blend of rational, emotional and instinctive responses to our environment. There is no better career choice than pursuing that which means the most to us.

SECTION 5:
REFLECTIONS

CHAPTER 5.1:

The Science and The Art

"Certain things catch your eye, but pursue only those that capture the heart."

– Native American proverb

In the previous chapters we have explored some of the insights and principles of neuroscience and, hopefully, this has presented us with a fresh view of what it means to be human. Yet it is an intriguing irony to me that science can throw so much light on life, which is essentially an art form. We live our lives as an entirely subjective experience. Of course, we have communication abilities which enable us to share thoughts and feelings at a rational or emotional level, but our instincts are our own, as is our DNA, uniquely available to us. And our memories are our own personal testimony to the life we have led and the sense we have tried to make of it. Our experience in the moment is itself unique and personal, as are our deepest reflections on life meaning and purpose.

Despite all this, science can offer significant insights into this experience and neuroscience has offered something new and exciting. For instance, it is crucial to understand that we are essentially energetic beings. Each of us is a human management system operating within the context of a wider universal energy system of which we are a part. Ignoring what goes on around us and concentrating only on what goes on inside us misses vital evidence in the search for continued understanding. We do not exist in a vacuum, our own development has been steered as a response to our environment and the environments we create and influence become significant factors in defining us.

Whilst the brain is the control centre of the human organism, the heart plays a significant role in our connectivity to the outside world and to those around us. The heart is also a big player in the creative process supporting both internal resonance and energetic flow. This is vital to artistic expression and interpretation. Whilst science seeks objective clarity and evidence, art is about creating a subjective experience. It is ours to interpret and feel and does not rely on corroboration with others. Art is about aesthetics, that which is pleasing to the senses.

Albert Einstein was probably the world's most famous scientist and there is no doubt that his reputation owed much to the rigour of his methods and the diligence of his approach. He left his brain to science and this revealed an extraordinarily large parietal lobe, the brain's region of complex rational thinking and problem solving. His ability to take his thinking into areas where others had not chosen to go and his expansive scientific deliberation truly deserved the label of genius. Yet a study of the man himself reveals the creative and intuitive talent that were likely to have been a crucial part of his exceptional intelligence,

"Imagination is more important than knowledge.

Knowledge is limited. Imagination encircles the world."

- Albert Einstein

Winston Churchill is remembered as a famous orator and passionate leader. Yet a visit to his former home, Chartwell House, clearly demonstrates how important his painting was to him. Churchill had the phenomenal capacity to both see and depict the big picture, whether he was painting on canvas or articulating another rousing speech. This ability to connect with his own deeper self and that of those around him elevated him as a very special human being.

Total intelligence is so much more than raw intellect. It is that fascinating blend of rationale, creativity and intuition that harnesses the potential of all our senses and capabilities. The deductive thinking of science can give us the route to clarity and reliable conclusions, whilst the inductive inspiration of creativity and art can create the pathways and breakthroughs that can enable fundamental changes in our lives. Each is as important as the other, invaluable jewels in the human crown. And perhaps the biggest jewel of all is the ability to see the bigger picture. Great leaders throughout history, whether spiritual or secular, have been able to invoke the images and meaning that strike us at the core of our deepest beliefs.

CHAPTER 5.2:

Spirituality and Belief

*"Always embrace the common humanity
that lies at the heart of us all."*

– Dalai Lama

Can neuroscience offer us a perspective on spirituality? I think the answer is yes. Of course, it cannot prove or disprove the existence of any divine being but it can present us with some insights into why this subject is of so much importance to us.

In the earlier pages of this book we have seen that belief is a matter of connection with our environment, the question of where we belong. If we see or sense an environment where we truly feel at home and at one with our purpose, we feel fulfilled and such an environment has a huge pull effect on our emotions and instincts. In simpler species, such as reptiles or mammals, this is likely to be the external environment, but in humans, whilst connection with our external environment can be inspiring and calming, such as the natural landscape of the countryside or the freedom of the sea, we look equally to our internalised environment to secure our beliefs.

The human brain is so intensely influenced by our reflective thought process that we search out an internalised interpretation for life meaning. Our experience as a human species has taught us not to accept the limitations of the immediate environment we see around us. Our curiosity drives us to look beyond such palpable boundaries and to think about what exists beyond. And when we contemplate what goes on beyond, we will always ask the broader question 'why?' Seeking out our purpose remains a vital ingredient of our human essence. In everyday life this is a matter of interpreting feedback from others to understand our impact on the world. Those around us act as mirrors to offer us a perspective on who we are. Yet, when we think about life beyond our world, we have to imagine entities or beings that may provide us with understanding and validation at this higher level. We know life exists beyond the boundaries of our physical world; we can simply look up at the night sky to observe its reality. This bigger picture holds a fascination for us, a sense of both awe and comfort to feel that we are a part of something bigger. How different it would be if we looked out solely on darkness!

This combination of purpose and curiosity provides the seeds for spiritual belief. I have had many conversations about this and have yet to meet someone who believes in nothing. Many people believe in God as the ultimate presence with whom to seek validation. Others may believe in Heaven on Earth, the concept which represents our ultimate and total fulfilment as a human species. Others will reject the idea of an ultimate presence and prefer to believe in concepts such as universal energy or life force, or even the rules of mathematics. We all need some explanation as to what life is about and I respect anyone's right to hold whatever belief is right for them.

Having said that, I believe there is less value to be gained from how our beliefs differentiate us and more from understanding why we all share the universal need to believe in something bigger than ourselves. Central to this understanding is the realisation that the human brain cannot contemplate 'nothingness'. Our brains are designed to fill in the gaps in our knowledge and this applies equally to matters of belief. Consider how we process the extremes of our understanding.

How can we contemplate what existed before the 'Big Bang', the point in time when our universe was created? We understand that there was a particular combination of gases and environmental conditions which caused the initial explosion which has resulted billions of years later in the universe we understand today. So where did these gases and environmental conditions come from? Who or what put them there? Have they always existed? If so, how can we contemplate 'always', the idea of no beginning and no end? We seek to understand everything from our own experience and we perceive our lives as having a distinct beginning and end. So concepts of the everlasting, whether spiritual or physical, sit entirely outside of our experience.

Another example is how we contemplate the biggest or the smallest. The biggest phenomenon that most of us relate to is the universe: it is the largest perceived reality within our human experience. So what exists beyond the universe? Is your brain hurting yet? And what of the smallest? We know that there is some fantastic experimentation going on now under the mountains of northern Europe to take our understanding of the fundamental blocks of human life to an even more microscopic level. But will we ever reach the end? Is there such a thing as the smallest or largest or are they more a reflection of the limits of human understanding at any one point in time? Does the concept of smallest or largest exist at all or are they simply dimensions which go on for ever?

Science cannot give us the answer to these big picture questions. It has to create rules and boundaries to progress with conviction. Yet for a brain that needs answers this is not enough. We are left with taking a leap of faith. For most of us, rationality alone fails to fill the void of ultimate human meaning. So we refer outwardly to others to give us these answers, such as religions and spiritualists, and we refer inwardly to our own internalised, imagined environment where we seek that ultimate sense of belonging and validation of the purpose of our lives.

For some it is a matter of submitting to the intuitive, for others it may be a submission to the rational. For me, there is no basis for one to be judgemental about the other. Religion cannot claim to have produced rational proof of a divine being; science cannot claim to have disproven the presence of divinity or to have captured and exercised the power of intuitive knowledge. These are parallel paths on the road of human discovery.

CHOICE

"Life can only be understood backwards,
but it must be lived forwards."

– Soren Kierkegaard

The study of neuroscience also confronts us with some very uncomfortable questions and top of this list is the matter of choice. Do we exercise any choice at all in the way we live and make sense of our lives? Whilst most of us will cling on to the emotional connection to our own will and ability to exercise choice, there is a plausible argument that challenges this. Our neurological template is created by our DNA. There is little doubt that this is unique to us and our subjective experience of life supports our sense of individuality. Yet it can reasonably be argued that our experience of life is entirely built on our pre-programmed responses to our environment and to the information we have available to us at the time.

The study of epigenetics is concerned with the expression of our genes throughout life. Our genes do not activate constantly but are turned on and off in response to environmental triggers. So we start life with our own unique predisposition to the challenges and opportunities we will encounter. Some of our genetic potential may never be triggered if our environments do not provide the stimulus. As life progresses, our responses are moulded as part of the cumulative lessons we learn but even these could be argued to be predetermined, that is the lessons we learn and the way we learn them are also pre-programmed. This makes me uncomfortable but I have to accept it might be true. Surely, part of life is confronting the uncomfortable if we are truly to learn?

This does not take anything away from our uniqueness. Our DNA is ours and ours alone and it is our life, whether chosen or predetermined. I have always been attracted to the snowflakes analogy. Despite their volume, each snowflake has its own unique design. Even if it has melted, when we refreeze each individual snowflake in the same environmental conditions it will reform according to its original design. This to me is wondrous and also poses an interesting parallel question. For each snowflake to be unique, something must have given it its original design. What was this? The original design must have either pre-existed or been created entirely by the unique combination of events at the point of its creation, or even a hybrid of both. So, what of the human parallel? Are we human snowflakes in the sense that our very unique essence already existed before we came to human life on Earth? Could we refer to this as our soul? Or were we entirely created by the unique conditions that existed at the point of our conception, and does this mean that if we cannot reverse time the point of conception cannot be recreated and so we cease to exist, even energetically, at the point of death?

If we examine the universal laws of physics which surround this conundrum, they offer further light. Although the parallel between snowflakes and humans may at first seem fanciful, we both exist within the same universe and there is a fair argument that the laws of creation apply equally to us both at the most basic molecular level. Furthermore, it is impossible to destroy energy, we can merely channel or transform it. Therefore the chances of us ceasing to exist in any energetic form after our lives seems illogical. The question then becomes do we retain our unique energetic design on an everlasting basis, such that we come back to 'life' when the appropriate conditions are recreated? Once again, could this be what many of us intuitively believe to be the 'soul'?

Or at the point of death do we revert back to become part of a wider universal energy rather like the wave returning to the ocean? Extending this latter analogy even further, the wave never entirely leaves the ocean and is only seen as an entity in its own right for the brief period of energetic flow which raises it to a level of part-separation from the main mass. Are we then waves briefly and partly separated from the universal ocean, and is our entire life spent trying to find our way back to the place we belong? If we are in any way energetically displaced or prised away from our former environment, it may explain why personal validation is such a driving force in our pursuit of life meaning.

And here is another angle: we readily accept that we are genetically created by our parents and our parents were themselves created by their parents, and so on throughout our ancestry. We are therefore directly linked by our bloodline to those that came before us. Does this not ultimately connect us to our original point of creation? Does this connection not extend back through both human and pre-human life so that eventually we are connected directly to the original source of our design? This argument certainly stands up in the physical sense of our molecular structure. So, if the original source of creation was a divine being, aren't we still directly connected at the deepest level to 'God'?

RELIGION AND FAITH

Spirituality can take many forms, as represented by the various religions which are in existence. Whilst spirituality reflects the beliefs we experience in our own inner lives, religion is more concerned with the expression of that belief and the practices that enable it to be shared.

My own upbringing could be loosely described as Christian; it has stayed with me throughout my life but my interpretation of its meaning is very subjective and does not lend itself to what I see as church ritual. I love churches but I prefer to be there when no one else is about. This does not mean that I judge church practice as negative; it clearly works for a lot of people and I respect that, and my experience of genuine Christians is very positive.

At the same time I have been blessed in my encounters with people from different religions. I lived amongst a Sikh community for a year when I was at university and found them to be warm, generous and welcoming. I was asked to speak at a Young Muslims Conference a few years ago and found spending time with them so rewarding. I had been stupid enough to leave my car lights on in the car park on a very frosty day, and when I returned to start my journey home after the evening dinner I was confronted with an extremely flat battery. Rather embarrassingly I asked if anyone could help and was then surrounded by what seemed the whole local Muslim community as they came out to help and made sure I was able to get on the road. It is so sad that such a loving community is tarred across the globe by the damage of extremists. More recently I have enjoyed deep discussions with those who follow the Hindu faith, whilst my personal study of Buddhism has offered me great richness in life.

My point here is that religious choices do not separate people into good or bad, neither does 'believing' or 'not believing'. Every one of us has the right to choose, albeit we will always be significantly influenced by our upbringing. Furthermore, experience has taught me that closer engagement with the people who follow the various religions reveals that at the human level we believe mostly in the same things. Religious beliefs may take a different form at the level of representation of the divine, as is clearly demonstrated across the divergence of faiths, but this does not alter our view about what we believe to be good as human practice. As codes of conduct, most religions (with only a few exceptional extremist interpretations) encourage love, understanding and mutual respect for one another.

Humans appear to share many common standards when it comes to morality, yet the history of religious practice clearly demonstrates how damaging it has been in dividing us. Many wars have been fought in the name of religion and it continues to cause tension and separation in many modern societies.

So, what does this have to do with neuroscience? I believe we can help people to understand why the need for spiritual belief is such a fundamental force in so many lives. We can explain the commonality rather than the separation.

I personally believe that we need to get beyond the differences of divine representation that cause so much strife. Too often, the standard religious assumption seems to be that their divine belief and the form it takes is the source point for all reason and argument; that everything begins and ends with their own view of God. It seems to me that along the way we have forgotten that our concepts of the divine have been created by humanity itself. The form our God takes reflects the environment and culture experienced by our ancestors. We have created our own images and then given them complete authority over us.

I am not representing this argument with any sense of negativity. Indeed, I am suggesting that the evolution and development of our brains gave us no choice but to do this. As discussed earlier, our understanding of the human brain tells us that we cannot conceive 'nothingness'. Therefore, to be able to connect with a divine belief, we would have to give that belief a tangible form. Invariably that form resembles our own human form, which is hardly surprising since that was what we knew. So, across the cultures of the world we created divine images in quasi-human form to support our beliefs. The communication and sharing of our beliefs depended heavily on the relative tangibility of these created images. It is difficult to imagine how churches or religious communities could be sustainable without such anchoring icons. Abstract concepts alone are not the foundation for shared religious practice.

Importantly, this argument should not be seen as a view which denies a divine presence. I am merely commenting on the necessity communities have faced in creating their own imagery that represented their beliefs. Each culture has found its own way in this. Nevertheless, there may still be a common underlying source of spirit or energy that underpins all of these beliefs. The fact that cultures have developed different religious images may not alter the consideration that their inspiration lies in one universal being or presence. This is the essence of belief; it is intuitive, something we sense or feel, it is not rational.

People's choices about the 'God' they believe in deserve complete respect, yet underneath there is a potential universality of belief in humanity itself which desperately needs to be nurtured. We appear to have given up faith in ourselves and referred it out instead to divine presences that can be neither proven nor disproven. Tension and angry judgement of the religious practice of others comes from one source alone, that of fear. When we meet others in a place of tolerance and respect we can see and feel what binds us and what brings us together. Maybe at times this has enabled us to abdicate responsibility for our own actions on Earth? Religious difference needs to be understood with tolerance, not divided by fear, and the human race needs to take back full responsibility for its actions.

CHAPTER 5.3:

What Does The Future Hold?

"Man has made many machines, complex and cunning,

but which of them indeed rivals the workings of his heart?"

– Pablo Casals

ARTIFICIAL INTELLIGENCE AND THE HUMAN TAKEOVER

There is a lot of press coverage at the moment on the subject of intelligent robots and their potential replacement of human intelligence. Are we indeed creating a robotic species which will become more powerful than ourselves?

It is a consideration which is both exciting and scary at the same time. History has shown us that inventions can be used or abused. Tools are there for deployment but until now humans have made the decisions around how they are to be used. But what if the advance of artificial intelligence created entities that could ignore human directives and simply decide for themselves? What if future robots had no regard for the survival of humanity and took it on themselves instead to focus their intelligence on the survival of their own species?

Whilst it would be crazy to say 'never', it is a prospect that is a lot further away than most literature suggests. These prophecies of doom are largely predicated on the premise that artificial intelligence will advance to such a level of sophistication that it will replace the human brain, as witnessed, for example, by well-known successes of AI machines over global chess masters. The reality, however, is that this is only one part of the story. As we have seen throughout this book, the human brain does not exist in isolation from the wider human intelligence system. AI itself may to some degree eventually be able to match the logical circuitry of the brain but human intelligence is so much more. Let's remind ourselves of some of these insights.

Human logical capability resides in the cortex, the outer and youngest region of the brain, the area where we have taken our thinking ability well beyond the levels of other living species. It is also the area which lends itself most to AI replication as it operates fundamentally on digital principles. Yet only 20% of human intelligence resides at this level; the rest sits at the unconscious level, and this covers both the limbic and basal regions of the brain.

The limbic region works on analogue principles. This means that it is state sensitive, for which the essential ingredient is energy. As humans we can sense each other's energy without any involvement from the logical brain. This limbic interchange is an essential part of human interaction, mutual understanding and social cooperation. So, robots of the future will not only need to possess logical capability, they will also need to be energetically sensitive.

And the challenge goes further. The limbic system of the brain has critical neural connections to the heart. The heart itself operates its own neurological system and is a vital partner to the brain in the conduct and experience of our lives. So, to really replace us, robots will need hearts as well as brains!

Then we have the basal layer of the brain, the reptilian brain, the home of our instincts. These instincts are derived from our genetic programming, in essence our DNA. Our DNA is nature's means of passing on through the generations the survival and development lessons learnt by our predecessors. They form a critical part of our intelligence system and our response to our environment. So now, to truly take up the banner of human replacement, robots will not only need to have hearts but also an evolutionary DNA which enables hereditary learning!

I don't think we need to worry too much for the moment.

THE FOURTH LAYER?

I suppose it is inevitable that when we look at the subject matter of this book, we look back on human evolution to date and assume a position of hindsight. Tangibility sits more readily in our past than our future, but what might the future hold for the development of the brain?

The triune brain model has been a cornerstone for this book, but why should evolution stop at three layers? Indeed, any suggestion that evolution will be satisfied to reach its destination at a particular place and time seems totally at odds with the evidence to date. So, why not a fourth layer of the brain? The third layer, the cortex, and in particular the pre-frontal cortex, has given us the capacity to take some control of our global environment, but what of our journey into the universe? Will our brains develop a fourth layer that gives us the capability to reach, travel and survive at an intergalactic level? Does the fourth layer already exist in embryonic form? Do we already have the ability to connect beyond our world;

is it simply that we have not yet discovered it? If this capacity sits entirely in energetic rather than physical form, maybe it is already there, waiting for us to tap into it?

POST SCRIPT:

Cancer

"If you get up one more time than you fall,
you will make it through."

– Chinese proverb

During the writing of this book, my life has taken an unwelcome turn as my partner, Sally, has been diagnosed with lymphoma cancer. The impact on her life has been brutal as she struggles to cope with the effects of a necessarily aggressive chemotherapy and radiotherapy regimen. Emotionally, she and I are being stretched to the limit and, for the moment at least, it feels like our lives have been permanently damaged.

We have had to do the best we can to try to get through this but the sense of devastation is not just for us; we have seen at first hand just how destructive it is to the people and families we encounter at the regular treatment sessions we have had to endure. My heart goes out to anyone facing a similar challenge.

Sally's prognosis is not yet clear so we continue to hope and pray for the best. Cancer may not be directly within the scope of this book but its appearance in our lives now becomes part of my life's journey. Such a significant event could not go unmentioned.

Additionally, it causes me to reflect on this apparently very modern disease. Of course, we have only had the diagnostic capability to recognise cancer over recent decades, but the scale of its expansion is very scary. It is like the modern plague.

We already know that there is a significant correlation between cancer and stress. It is not a causal link. We know that some of us carry a genetic disposition towards developing cancer but it seems that stress can be one of the triggers that kick it into action. Our bodies have learnt to cope with episodic stress but modern society often throws up the challenge of constant stress. This could be the pressure of trying to keep up with the demands of a job, of balancing home life and work, or keeping up with our peers in the self-induced race for material possessions. The consequence of this is relentless stress demanding more of our internal resources than we have to offer. This results over time in our bodies breaking down. Cancer is, after all, a condition where rogue cells turn on our good cells.

My thoughts are currently more preoccupied with Sally but there is also a bigger question here that we ignore at our peril. So many people in the western world are chasing material gain without fulfilling the need for meaning in their lives. There is a spiritual vacuum. Religion has been rubbished in so many quarters yet the need for spiritual meaning remains a cornerstone of purposeful lives. We all need to feel we are part of something bigger and meaningful.

This is especially significant for our younger generations who have grown up in a world of material access and the immediate availability of the internet and social media. Yet, in my experience these same generations are increasingly turning to their own search for meaning. As religious commitment weakens, phenomena like mindfulness are becoming increasingly popular but I sense that this is only a respite rather than a sustainable solution. I feel that we need to look first and foremost to ourselves for the answer. Yes there is the inner soul-searching which can be healthy for all of us but there is a bigger leap we can all make collectively. If we fully understand the design of our brains and the evolutionary purpose which drives it we can start to really explore our full potential as a social species. The search for collective tolerance and mutual understanding can take us to a place where we can offer each other all the validation, fulfilment and meaning that we need, a true Heaven on Earth.

"Our faith is kindness."

– Dalai Lama

RECOMMENDED READING LIST

The brain

Book	Author	Content
Social: Why our brains are wired to connect	Matthew Lieberman	The brain and relationships
Mindsight	Daniel Siegel	The science of kindness
The Emotional Brain	Joseph Ledoux	The inner workings of our emotional brain
The Inner Game of Tennis	Tim Gallwey	Human performance mastery
Blink	Malcolm Gladwell	The subconscious mind and 'thin-slicing'
Emotions Revealed	Paul Ekman	Instinctive and cultural behaviour
Emotional Intelligence	Daniel Goleman	Intro to emotional intelligence
Thinking Fast and Slow	Daniel Kahneman	The fast and slow thinking brain
Neuropsychology for Coaches	Paul Brown & Virginia Brown	Using neuroscience as coaches
Connectome	Sebastian Seung	The wiring of the brain
Why Men Don't Listen and Women Can't Read Maps	Alan and Barbara Pease	Gender differences

The heart

Book	Author	Content
The Heartmath Institute	Website, books, journals	Introduction to neurocardiology

About the Author

Having been brought up in the South Wales valleys and educated at Pontllanfraith Grammar School, Clive went on to study sociology at Warwick University. He then embarked initially on a Human Resources career, which lasted for about 12 years, before switching to business management. There then followed a series of leadership roles in large corporate organisations before becoming the CEO of an IT outsourcing company.

In 2005, Clive returned to coaching and has worked since then primarily with business leaders and their teams addressing strategic and cultural challenges. He also runs masterclass programmes for coaches, trainers, HR and Learning and Development practitioners. Additionally, he has coached in sport, education, public services, charities, prisons and faith organisations